Maths

GCSE

Liz Hamilton

What this book contains

$$x = \frac{-b \pm \sqrt{b^2 - (4ac)}}{(2a)}$$

How to do Rapid Revision

The aim of *Rapid Revision* is simple. It's to help you do better in your exam in a very short time. This book is for active revision – it puts you in charge. In order to do well in your exams you need to:

- have a plan of what you need to know – that's the Action plan on page 4
- quickly target what you need to learn – that's in the Revision units which are at the heart of this book
- be able to learn quickly and effectively
- understand what the examiners are looking for – that's in the grade-boosting tips in the answers

A few other things you need to know

What exam are you doing for GCSE Maths

You will be studying for GCSE Maths at one of three levels or tiers.

- For the Higher tier, the grades available are A*, A, B and C.
- For the Intermediate tier, the grades available are B, C D and E.
- For the Foundation tier, the grades available are D, E, F and G.

If you are aiming for a G, F or E grade, you will be advised to enter for the Foundation tier. If you are aiming for a D or C grade, you will be advised to enter for the Intermediate tier. The B grade is not so clear-cut. The usual advice is to enter for the Intermediate or Higher, but it is generally thought that it is easier to gain a B grade on the Intermediate paper. If you are aiming for an A or A* you must take the Higher paper.
For each tier you will be taking **two written papers**.
In year 2000, for the first time, **the first paper** in each tier is a **non-calculator paper**.
You will also be taking a **third written paper**, or doing **coursework** in your own time.
This is to test your skill in 'Using and applying Maths'.

What does this book cover?

This book covers all the Maths you need to know to achieve a B grade.
Topics 1–11 make up to 50% of the marks, topics 12–18 make up 25% of the marks and topics 19–22 make up the remaining 25% of the marks. If you are really short of time, you can see that it makes sense to concentrate on topics 19–22, as this relatively small section carries proportionately more marks.
If you are taking the Intermediate paper this book will help you to turn a D into a C or a C into a B. If you are doing the Higher tier there are extra topics you will need to revise, but this book will still give you lots of valuable revision practice.

Throughout the book, you will find boxes like this at the ends of topics.

Key facts and skills

- **for density**: $M = D \times V$, $D = M \div V$, $V = M \div D$
- **for speed**: $D = S \times T$, $S = D \div T$, $T = D \div S$
- in **compound measures** 'per' means divide

These Key Facts and Skills boxes are useful summaries of what you have to know to do well. It is worth writing these facts onto revision cards to carry around with you until you are completely sure you know them. There are also some Tips boxes which should help you avoid common errors or help you when you are solving problems.

Don't forget to look at the secrets of success in maths on page 6.

How to get going

Step 1

Look at the action plan on page 4. Check on what you need to know. You can start with the first item on the list or you can target something that worries you.

Step 2

Choose a revision unit. The revision units are in three parts:

1 The Check Up

How well do you know the topic? Do this quick check to find out. If it seems OK you can skip The Crash Course and go straight to the Exam Practice Questions – or you can go straight on to another unit. Rapid revision means targeting what you need to learn. It's very easy to spend time on things you already know!

2 The Crash Course

That's the bit which teaches you the key facts and skills you must know to do well in the exam. It puts the essential facts and knowledge very clearly and simply – and it's broken into small chunks for easy learning.

3 The Exam Practice

These provide GCSE type questions section by section. They are a real test of what you need to know in the exam. Answers to all the questions come with grade-boosting tips.

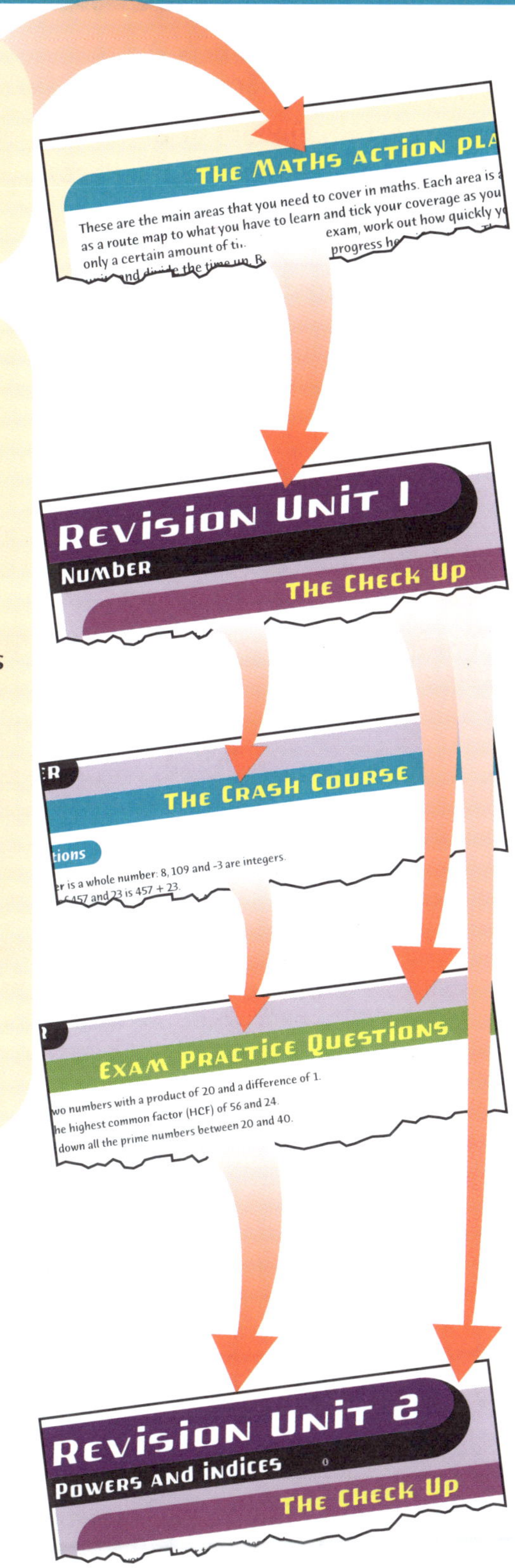

The revision units are really flexible – if you want, just do the crash courses to get the facts – or focus on exam practice close to the exams

Step 3

Record your progress on the action plan if you want. Then go on to the next unit.

And if you're really short of time …

1 Don't panic.
2 Do The Check Ups. Start with the topics you're less confident about. If you do OK, go straight to the next unit. If not, do The Crash Course.
3 Write the key things from The Crash Course you want to remember in note form on cards and pin them to your bedroom wall.
4 Don't try to learn anything new the night before the exam as you may just become muddled.

The Maths action plan

These are the main areas that you need to cover in maths. Each area is a revision unit. Use this as a route map to what you have to learn and tick your coverage as you go along. If you have only a certain amount of time before the exam, work out how quickly you need to cover the units and divide the time up. Record your progress here if you like. Then concentrate on the units you're least confident about.

You might like to start your action plan by finding out and recording:

Dates of exams

Tier (level) you're entered for
Foundation / Intermediate / Higher

Unit	How many times revised			Check up score	Exam Practice score	Areas in which you feel you need more practice
	1	2	3			
1 Number X						
2 Powers and indices						
3 Percentages X						
4 Ratio, conversions and compound measure						
5 Algebra X						
6 Linear equations and formulae						

7 Factorising and quadratics ×						
8 Plotting and using graphs						
9 Gradients and lines ×						
10 Solving more equations ×						
11 Sequences ×						
12 Angles and lines						
13 Transformations ×						
14 Loci						
15 Triangles						
16 Trigonometry ×						
17 Length and area						
18 3D shapes ×						
19 Data						
20 Averages and ranges						
21 Scatter diagrams ×						
22 Probability ×						

The secrets of sucess in Maths

Make an action plan, starting well in advance.

Two months before the exam

Plan your revision

You must make sure that you plan your revision carefully.
Then try to stick to your plan.

Practice questions

It is important to do as many practice questions as possible, to make sure you understand the work you have revised.

One week before the exam

Check that you have all the correct equipment

You will need a pen, sharp pencil, pencil sharpener, rubber, ruler, protractor and compasses.
Remember, on the first paper you will not be allowed a calculator.
For the second paper you will need a calculator. If it needs batteries, make sure they are new and that your calculator works. For any work in trigonometry you will be working in degrees, so make sure your calculator is operating in degree mode.

The day before each exam

You don't want to be tired for the exam, so make sure you get enough sleep.
Revision at this stage will probably not help - in fact it could be counter-productive.

Exam day

Check your equipment again - only take what you are allowed to have with you in the exam.
Remember that you can ask the invigilator for tracing paper, to help with questions on transformations.

What do you have to do to succeed in the actual exams? Here are ten key points to remember.

1. You must make sure you have the correct paper. Mistakes have been known to happen. Make sure that the first thing you do is fill in the front page correctly, with your name, your candidate number and the centre number.
2. Remember that you will have been entered at the tier that is appropriate for you, so you should be confident that you will be able to do the exam well.
3. You must read each question carefully, think how you would work out the answer, then check that you are doing what you have been asked.
4. Work through the paper steadily. You must not spend too much time on any one question. The marks given for each question are clearly shown. For example, if a question is worth 5 marks, don't spend more than five or six minutes on it.
5. If you get stuck on a question, put a mark by it and come back to it later.
6. Make sure that you try to answer all the questions. If you only answer three-quarters of all the questions, you can only get three-quarters of the marks, at most.
7. Don't lose marks by not showing all your working. In most questions, marks are given specifically for the method and separate marks are given for the answer.
8. Remember to write the answer to the order of accuracy asked. If you are not given a number of places to which you should round, look at the numbers in the question and use a similar degree of accuracy.
9. Add lines to diagrams, if it helps. This is especially true for questions on angles or graphs.
10. Take care with the scales on graphs. The scales on the vertical and the horizontal axes are often different.

Revision Unit 1

Number

The Check Up

1 Round these numbers.

a) 159 to the nearest 100 ____________

b) 156.4 to the nearest whole number ____________

c) 236.74 to 1 d.p. ____________

d) 166.666 666 666 to 2 d.p. ____________

e) 2.889 to 3 s.f. ____________

f) 21 543 to 2 s.f. ____________

g) 0.000 168 9 to 1 s.f. ____________

2 From the following list
2, 3, 4, 5, 6, 7, 8, 9, 10, 11, 12, 13, 14, 15
pick out:

a) all the prime numbers ____________

b) all the triangular numbers ____________

c) the multiples of 3 ____________

d) the factors of 15 ____________

3 Write 1890 as a product of its prime factors. ____________

4 Use your calculator to find the value of $\frac{32.7 \times 19.3}{18.97 - 9.38}$.
Write down your answer in full, then round your answer to 3 significant figures. ____________ ____________

Check your answer using numbers rounded to 1 significant figure. ____________

5 The length of a metal bar is measured to be 13.26 cm.

What is the least possible length of the bar? ____________

What is the greatest possible length of the bar? ____________

6 The number of people at a garden fete was given as 2600, to the nearest hundred.

Write down the maximum and minimum number of people at the fair. ____________ ____________

Mark yourself *(see answers on page 98)*

- Just a few wrong? You're geared up for the Exam Practice Questions. Go for it!
- More than a few wrong? Boost your learning powers by taking the Crash Course before you tackle the Exam Practice Questions.

/19

The Crash Course

Definitions

An **integer** is a whole number: 8, 109 and -3 are integers.
The **sum** of 457 and 23 is 457 + 23 = 480.
The **difference** between 457 and 23 is 457 − 23 = 434.
The **product** of 457 and 23 is 457 × 23 = 10 511.
The **triangular numbers** are made by adding **consecutive** numbers.
Start with **1**, then 1 + 2 = **3**, then 1 + 2 + 3 = **6**, then 1 + 2 + 3 + 4 = **10**…
Factors are numbers which divide into another number exactly.
The factors of 12 are 1, 2, 3, 4, 6 and 12.
The **highest common factor** (HCF) of two numbers is the largest number that is a factor of both.
Multiples of a number have that number as a factor.
The multiples of 7 are 7, 14, 21, 28, 35…
The **lowest common multiple** (LCM) of two numbers is the smallest number that is a multiple of both.
A **prime number** is a number which has only two factors (1 and itself).
The prime numbers are 2, 3, 5, 7, 11, 13, 17, 19, 23, 29, 31…

Tip:
1 is not a prime number because it has only one factor.

How to find the prime factors of a number

Start by dividing by the lowest prime number (2) until it will not divide exactly any more. Then do the same with the next prime number (3), then the next (5) and so on.

Example

Write 350 as a product of its prime factors.
Divide 350 by the smallest prime number (2) until it will not divide any more.
350 ÷ 2 = 175 — 350 = 2 × 175
Now try the next smallest prime number (3): 175 ÷ 3 won't divide exactly.
Now try 5: 175 ÷ 5 = 35 — 350 = 2 × 5 × 35
As 35 is a multiple of 5, try 5 again: 35 ÷ 5 = 7 — 350 = 2 × 5 × 5 × 7
This leaves the prime number 7.
The prime factors of 350 are 2, 5 and 7.
Written as a product of its prime factors, $350 = 2 \times 5 \times 5 \times 7 = 2 \times 5^2 \times 7$

How to round numbers

Numbers can be rounded to a given degree of accuracy, such as the nearest hundred, the nearest ten, the nearest whole number, to 1, 2, 3… decimal places or significant figures.
The rounding rule is: if the number in the **next** place is 5 or more round up, if it is less than 5 round down.

How to round whole numbers

The height of Helvellyn is 3118 feet. Write this to the nearest hundred feet.
Look at the digit in the place after 'hundreds'. The digit in the 'tens' place is 1 so round down.
3118 ft is 3100 ft (to the nearest 100).

How to round numbers using decimal places

- Write 3.86 correct to one decimal place (d.p.).
  To round to one decimal place, look at the next (second) decimal place which is 6.
  This is greater than 5 so round up. 3.86 is 3.9 (to 1 d.p.).
- Write 4.6745 to two decimal places.
  To round to two decimal places, look at the next (third) decimal place which is 4.
  This is less than 5 so round down. 4.6745 is 4.67 (to 2 d.p.).

The Crash Course

Significant figures

Counting from the left, the first **non-zero** number is the first significant figure (s.f.). The next number is always the second significant figure, and so on.

How to round numbers using significant figures

- Write 43.57 correct to three significant figures.
  To round to three significant figures, look at the fourth significant figure which is 7: round up. 43.57 is 43.6 (to 3 s.f.).
- Write 0.002 353 correct to one significant figure.
  The first significant figure is the 2, so the second significant figure is 3: round down. 0.002 353 is 0.002 (to 1 s.f.).
- Write 108.6 correct to two significant figures.
  To round to two significant figures, look at the third significant figure which is 8: round up. 108.6 is 110 (to 2 s.f.)
  Remember to put in a zero to make the number the correct size.

How to check calculations

Significant figures can be used to estimate and check calculations. To 1 s.f. 2.8 = 3, 4.7 = 5 and 3.61 = 4.

$\frac{2.8}{4.7 + 3.61} \approx \frac{3}{5 + 4} \approx \frac{3}{9} \approx 0.3$ which about the same as the calculated value found in the example below.

How to use the calculator memory or brackets

Key **Min** to put a number in the memory. Key MR to get the number out of the memory.

Example

Work out $\frac{2.8}{4.7 + 3.61}$ Use either the calculator memory or brackets.

- Using memory: Key: **4** **.** **7** **+** **3** **.** **6** **1** **=** **Min**. Now key: **2** **.** **8** **÷** **MR**
  Calculator displays the answer: 0.3369
- Using brackets: Key: **2** **.** **8** **÷** **(** **4** **.** **7** **+** **3** **.** **6** **1** **)** **=**
  Calculator displays the answer: 0.3369

Tip:
Check your own calculator.

Tip:
Do not key: 2.8 ÷ 4.7 + 3.61
which works out $\frac{2.8}{4.7} + 3.61$

Errors

Suppose Cath's height to the nearest whole number is 194 cm.
Then Cath's height can be anywhere between 193.5 cm and less than 194.5 cm.
The maximum error in Cath's height is 1 cm ÷ 2 = 0.5 cm

Example

Clare's weight is 81.7 kg. Find Clare's smallest and largest weight.
Clare's weight is given to 1 d.p. This means the maximum error is 0.1 kg ÷ 2 = 0.05 kg
Her smallest weight is 81.7 − 0.05 kg = 81.65 kg
Her largest weight is less than 81.7 + 0.05 kg = 81.75 kg

Key facts and skills

- a **integer** is a whole number
- a **prime number** has two factors only (1 and itself)
- **round numbers** to the nearest hundred, ten, whole number, 1, 2 or 3 **decimal places**
- round numbers to 1, 2, 3... **significant figures**
- use **calculator keys**, including brackets and memory, when working out difficult divisions
- **use estimates to check answers** by writing numbers to 1 s.f.
- **maximum error** is half the number's lowest place value; error in a number to 2 d.p. is 0.01 ÷ 2 = 0.005

Exam Practice Questions

1 a) Find two numbers with a product of 20 and a difference of 1.

b) Find the highest common factor (HCF) of 56 and 24.

c) Write down all the prime numbers between 20 and 40.

2 The acceleration due to gravity g, is 9.807 m/s^2. Write this:

a) correct to 2 d.p.

b) correct to 2 s.f.

3 A window is measured as 1.342 m high and 1.152 m wide, each to the nearest tenth of a centimetre.

a) What are the largest possible height and width of the window?

b) What are the smallest possible height and width of the window?

4 Tameen hires a car to make a journey of 625 miles. The car averages 1 litre of petrol every 8.8 miles. Petrol costs $0.94 a litre and $1 = £0.67. By making suitable approximations estimate how much the petrol for the journey will cost in pounds.
Show your approximations and workings. Do not use a calculator.

5 Ed finishes a race in 3 minutes 21.46 seconds. What is the shortest time he could have taken?

Revision Unit 2

Powers and indices

The Check Up

1 Use your calculator to work these out. Give answers to 2 d.p. where necessary.

a) $4^6 - 6^2$ ______

b) $3^{-3} + 2^{-3}$ ______

c) $(0.041)^2$ ______

d) $\sqrt{\dfrac{2.36 \times 18.47}{7.19 - 1.33}}$ ______

2 Do **not** use your calculator to work these out.

a) $(2^2)^3$ Give the answer in index form. ______

b) 5^0 ______

c) $4^{-1} - 3^{-2}$ ______

d) $3^{-2} \times 3^3$ ______

e) $5^3 \div 5^2$ ______

3 a) The distance of Mars from the sun is 227 900 000 km.

Write this in standard form. ______

b) The mass of a grain of sand is 0.000 000 004 2 g.

Put this in standard form. ______

4 a) The mass of an atom of carbon is 1.66×10^{-12} kg.
Calculate the mass of 8×10^{24} atoms of carbon. Give your answer in standard form, correct to 2 d.p.

______

b) $C = 3 \times 10^{-4}$ and $D = 2 \times 10^{-5}$. Calculate
$C - D$ and $C \div D$ giving your answers in standard form. ______ ______

5 a) A square has an area of 12 cm^2.
What is the length of a side? Give your answer to 1 d.p. ______

b) A cube has a volume of 16 cm^3.
Find the length of a side of the cube, giving your answer to 3 s.f. ______

Mark yourself *(see answers on page 98)*

- *Just a few wrong?* You're geared up for the Exam Practice Questions. Go for it!
- *More than a few wrong?* Boost your learning powers by taking the Crash Course before you tackle the Exam Practice Questions.

/ 16

THE CRASH COURSE

Definitions

3^4 means $3 \times 3 \times 3 \times 3 = 81$
Say 'three to the power of four'. The '4' is the **index**. The plural of index is **indices**.

Square and cube numbers

The square numbers are:
$1^2 = 1$, $2^2 = 4$, $3^2 = 9$, $4^2 = 16$ and so on.
The cube numbers are:
$1^3 = 1$, $2^3 = 8$, $3^3 = 27$, $4^3 = 64$ and so on.

How to use a calculator with whole number indices

To work out 6.9^2 key: **6** **.** **9** **x²** The calculator displays the answer: 47.61
To work out 1.2^5 key: **1** **.** **2** **xʸ** **5** **=** The calculator displays the answer: 2.48832

Tip:
Check how your own calculator works out indices.
Some calculators may have a **yˣ** key, and some may need the shift or 2nd function key.

Zero index

Any number to the power of 0 is 1.
So $5^0 = 1$ and $10\,000\,002^0 = 1$.

Negative indices

A negative index always gives the reciprocal which means that it 'turns the fraction upside-down'.

7 can be written as $\frac{7}{1}$ so 7^{-1} (the negative index turns the fraction upside-down) $= \frac{1}{7}$.

10^{-4} (the negative index turns the number upside-down) $= \frac{1}{10^4}$ (the four raises to the power of 4)

$$= \frac{1}{10\,000}$$

How to use a calculator with negative whole number indices

To work out 3^{-4} key: **3** **xʸ** **4** **+/−** **=** The calculator displays the answer: 0.0123 …

The rules of indices

Adding and subtracting

Work out each term and then add or subtract.
$4^3 + 2^5 = 64 + 32 = 96$

Multiplying powers

To multiply different powers of the **same** number **add** the **indices**.
$2^4 \times 2^2 = 2^{4+2} = 2^6 = 64$ but $2^2 \times 5^3 = 4 \times 125$
$= 500$

Dividing powers

To divide different powers of the **same** number **subtract** the **indices**.
$2^2 \div 2^3 = 2^{2-3} = 2^{-1} = \frac{1}{2}$ but $2^2 \div 5^3 = 4 \div 125 = \frac{4}{125}$

Raising powers to a power

To raise a power of a number to a power multiply the indices.
$(5^2)^3 = 5^{2 \times 3} = 5^6 = 15\,625$

How to multiply and divide by powers of 10 without using a calculator

Multiplying by 10^3 appears to move the decimal point three places → → → to the right. $4567.0 \times 10^3 = 4\,567\,000$

Dividing by 10^2 appears to move the decimal point two places ← ← to the left. $4567.0 \div 10^2 = 45.67$

The Crash Course

Standard form

Standard form is a neat way to write very large numbers or very small numbers.
A number in standard form is written as (a base number) × (a power of 10).
The base number takes a value of 1 or greater, but less than 10.

Steps for writing a number in standard form

1. Find the first non-zero digit in the number. Put the decimal point after this digit. This gives the base number.
2. Count how many places the decimal point has 'moved'. This is the 'power of 10'. Remember it will be positive if the original number is greater than 10, or negative if the original number is less than 1. If the original number is already between 1 and 10, the power will be 0.

- Write 135.0 in standard form.
  1. The first non-zero digit is 1, so write the number as 1.35.
  2. The decimal point has 'moved' 2 places ← ← (135.0). The power of 10 is 2 (10^2). 135.0
     In standard form $135.0 = 1.35 \times 10^2$
- Write 0.000 72 in standard form.
  1. The first non-zero digit is 7 so write the number as 7.2.
  2. The decimal point has 'moved' 4 places → → → → (0.000 72). The power of 10 is −4 (10^{-4}). 0.00072
     In standard form $0.000\,72 = 7.2 \times 10^{-4}$

Calculators and numbers in standard form

Key in the base number, then enter the power of 10 by using the **EXP** key.

> **Tip:**
> Some calculators have an EE key instead of the EXP key. Some do not need the key. Check yours!

Examples

- To enter 4.7×10^4 on a calculator, key: **4** **·** **7** **EXP** **4** The calculator displays 4.7^{04} which means 4.7×10^4.
- To work out $2.3 \times 10^{-7} \times 3.9 \times 10^{-5}$ on a calculator, key: **2** **·** **3** **EXP** **7** **+/−** **×** **3** **·** **9** **EXP** **5** **+/−** **=**

  The calculator displays the answer 8.97^{-12} which means 8.97×10^{-12}.

Square and cube roots

Square root $\sqrt{\ }$ $\sqrt{25} = 5$ The square root of 25 is 5 ($25 = 5 \times 5$)
Cube root $\sqrt[3]{\ }$ $\sqrt[3]{8} = 2$ The cube root of 8 is 2 ($8 = 2 \times 2 \times 2$)

Example

Find the length (x) of a side of a cube of volume 10 cm³.
The volume of the cube is x^3 $x^3 = 10$ so $x = \sqrt[3]{10}$
To work this out key: **1** **0** **$\sqrt[3]{\ }$** The calculator displays the answer: 2.154 …
The length of a side of the cube is 2.15 cm (2 d.p.).

Key facts and skills

- **indices are powers of a number** and can be positive (e.g. $4^3 = 64$) or negative (e.g. $10^{-1} = 0.1$)
- **any number to the power of 0** (zero index) is 1
- to **multiply different powers of the same number add** the indices
- to **divide different powers of the same number subtract** the indices
- to **raise a power to a power multiply** the indices
- a number can be written in **standard form** as (base number) × (a power of 10)
- the **base number** takes a value of 1 or greater, but less than 10
- **use the EXP (or EE) calculator key** in calculations involving standard form
- use the $\sqrt{\ }$ key for **square roots** and the $\sqrt[3]{\ }$ key for **cube roots**

Exam Practice Questions

1 Use a calculator to work out the value of each of these. Give your answer in standard form, to 2 d.p.

a) $(0.0023)^2$

b) 2.34^3

c) 1.34^{-2}

d) $\sqrt[3]{20.5}$

2 Simplify the following expressions. Do not use a calculator.

a) $3^2 \times 3^5$ Leave your answer in index form.

b) $4^{-1} \times 4^3$

c) $2^6 \div 2^4$

d) $(2^3)^3$ Leave your answer in index form.

e) $3^6 \div 9^2$

3 Written as a product of its prime factors, $816 = 2^x \times 3 \times y$.
Find x and y.

4 Express the following in standard form.

a) The speed of light $c = 299\,800\,000$ m/s.

b) The gravitational constant $G = 0.000\,000\,000\,067$.

5 Use a calculator to work out $\dfrac{3.96 \times \sqrt{4.13}}{7.75 \times 1.43}$.
Write down the calculator answer in full. Then give the answer correct to 3 d.p.

6 Use a calculator to work out $\dfrac{2.15 \times 10^5}{7\,500\,000}$.
Give the answer in standard form to 3 d.p.

7 The volume of the sun is 1.31×10^{18} km^3. Its mass is 1.99×10^{30} kg.
What is its density? (density = mass per unit volume)
Give the answer to 2 d.p.

Revision Unit 3
Percentages

The Check Up

1 Write the following as percentages.

a) $\frac{5}{12}$ ______ b) 0.74 ______

2 In a class of 35, $\frac{3}{5}$ are girls. How many are girls? ______

3 A holiday costs £570. If travel expenses make up 45% of the total cost,

how much is spent on travel? ______

4 It costs £21 to repair Jill's bike and VAT at 17.5% is added to the bill.

How much is the total bill? ______

5 Find the simple interest on £3500 invested for 5 years at 3.50%. ______

6 A car cost £6420 new. It loses 12% of its current value each year.
How much is the car worth after 3 years?
Give your answer to an appropriate order of accuracy. ______

7 In a test Liz answered 18 questions correctly. This was 60% of the total

number of questions. How many questions were there in the test? ______

8 Prices of goods in a sale are reduced by 20%. In the sale Becky pays £12

for a T-shirt. Work out the original cost and how much she saves. ______ ______

9 In September it rained on 12 days. Write this as a fraction of the total

number of days in September. ______

10 Raj scored 153 marks out of 175. What is his percentage score, to 1 d.p.? ______

11 Cathy bought a hat for £50 then sold it to a friend for £35.

What was her percentage loss? ______

Mark yourself *(see answers on page 98)*

- Just a few wrong? You're geared up for the Exam Practice Questions. Go for it!
- More than a few wrong? Boost your learning powers by taking the Crash Course before you tackle the Exam Practice Questions.

/13

THE CRASH COURSE

Percentages and fractions

Per cent means per 100 or divide by 100.
So 37% means 37 per 100 or 37 out of 100 or $\frac{37}{100}$ or 0.37

How to change fractions or decimals into percentages

Multiply the fraction or decimal by 100.
$\frac{3}{8} = \frac{3}{8} \times 100\% = 37.5\%$ and $0.53 = 0.53 \times 100\% = 53\%$

How to calculate a percentage or fraction of a quantity

To find a percentage or fraction 'of', multiply the quantity by the percentage or fraction.
Remember, for 'of' read 'multiply'.

9% of 300 = $\frac{9}{100} \times 300 = 27$ On a calculator, key: 9 ÷ 1 0 0 × 3 0 0 =

$\frac{7}{8}$ of 60 = $\frac{7}{8} \times 60 = 52.5$ On a calculator, key: 7 ÷ 8 × 6 0 =

Tip: If your calculator has one, you can use the fraction button.

How to find a percentage increased or decreased value

First find the actual increase or decrease. Then add or subtract this from the original value.

EXAMPLE

After one year a bike which cost £350 is sold at a loss of 7%. What is the selling price?
Loss (decrease) is 7% of £350 = $\frac{7}{100}$ × £350 = £24.50
The price has **decreased** so selling price is £350 − £24.50 = £325.50

Simple interest

Simple interest is paid **only** on the original amount (the **principal**) each year.

EXAMPLE

Lee's bank account pays 3.25% simple interest per annum (each year). Find out how much interest he earns on £2000 invested for 4 years.
First year's interest is 3.25% of £2000 = $\frac{3.25}{100}$ × £2000 = £65
For 4 years the interest is £65 × 4 = £260

Compound interest

Compound interest is paid on the **total amount** each year.
To calculate compound interest, find the interest for the first year. Then add this interest to the original amount and find the interest on this new amount for the second year, and so on.

EXAMPLE

Find the compound interest on £150 invested for 3 years at 4.5% p a.
First year's interest is $\frac{4.5}{100}$ × £150 = £6.75 New amount is £150 + £6.75 = £156.75
Second year's interest is $\frac{4.5}{100}$ × £156.75 = £7.05 New amount is £156.75 + £7.05 = £163.80
Third year's interest is $\frac{4.5}{100}$ × £163.80 = £7.37
For 3 years the total interest is £6.75 + £7.05 + £7.37 = £21.17

Tip: Read each problem carefully to decide if the percentage increase (or decrease) is worked on the original amount or the original amount plus the increase (or minus decrease) each year.

The Crash Course

Compound interest and multiplying factors

Working out compound interest for a large number of years can be tedious. It is quicker to use a **multiplying factor**.

Example

Nicola invests £150 at 4% per annum compound interest.
How much will she have after 6 years?
The interest is 4% so the multiplying factor is $1 + 0.04 = 1.04$
After 1 year she will have $£150 \times 1.04$
After two years she will have $£150 \times 1.04 \times 1.04 = £150 \times (1.04)^2$
So after 6 years she will have $£150 \times (1.04)^6 = £189.80$ to the nearest penny.

Tip:

Remember that the whole is 100%, the interest is 4% so the amount after a year will be 104%, and 104% is the same as 1.04.

'Backwards percentages'

These questions give the actual increased or decreased quantity and ask for the original quantity. To find the original quantity, divide the given increased or decreased quantity by the appropriate percentage.

Examples

- In a tin of fruit drops 35% are orange flavour. Nell found there were 28 orange. How many fruit drops were in the tin?
  35% of the number of fruit drops is 28
  1% of the number of fruit drops is $28 \div 35$
  100% of the number of fruit drops is $28 \div 35 \times 100 = 80$
  So the number of fruit drops in the tin was 80.
- A boutique makes 93% profit on each garment sold. How much did the boutique pay for a dress they sell for £145.00?
  Profit is increase so the selling price is $(100 + 93)\% = 193\%$ of the cost price.
  193% of the cost price is £145.00
  1% of the cost price is $£145.00 \div 193$
  100% of the cost price is $£145.00 \div 193 \times 100 = £75.13$ (2 d.p.)
  The price the boutique paid (original price or cost price) is £75.13.

One quantity as a fraction or percentage of another quantity

Put the first quantity as a fraction of the second, taking care to use the same units.
Then to find the percentage, multiply the fraction by 100.

Examples

- I spend 25 minutes of my homework time of 2 hours on Maths. What fraction of my homework time is spent on Maths?
  Work in minutes:
  2 hours = 2×60 minutes = 120 minutes.
  The fraction is $\frac{25}{120} = \frac{5}{24}$ (Divide 'top' and 'bottom' by 5.)
  The percentage is $\frac{5}{24} \times 100 = 20.8\%$ (1 d.p.)
- The population of a small island increases from 689 to 712. What is the percentage increase in population?
  Actual increase is $712 - 689 = 23$
  Percentage increase is $\frac{\text{actual change}}{\text{original amount}} \times 100\%$
  $= \frac{23}{689} \times 100\% = 3.3\%$ (1 d.p.)

Key Facts and Skills

- to find a percentage of a quantity **multiply** the quantity by the percentage
- **simple interest** is paid on the same amount each year
- **compound interest** is paid on (previous amount + interest) each year
- to find an original quantity ('backwards percentages') **divide** the quantity by the percentage
- **percentage change** is $\frac{\text{actual change}}{\text{original amount}} \times 100\%$

Exam Practice Questions

1 Copy this table and fill it in.

Percentage	Decimal	Fraction
5%		
		$\frac{3}{8}$
	0.55	

2 Work out the cost of the trainers which are advertised as shown.

a) Pre-sale price £55. Now in the sale with 18% reduction.

b) Selling price £45 plus 17.5% VAT.

c) Usual price £76. Now in the sale at $\frac{2}{3}$ of usual price.

3 A CD album is reduced from £15.60 to £12.50.
What is the percentage reduction? Give your answer to the nearest whole number.

4 In Highwood school 108 pupils walk to school. This is 27% of all the pupils. How many pupils are there in the school?

5 A student sells his revision books for £45 which is a loss of 30% on the price he paid for them. How much did he originally pay for his books?

6 Jo buys a flat for £45 000. He reckons the flat will increase in value by 7% each year. If his prediction is correct how much will the flat be worth in:

a) 1 year

b) 3 years

c) 20 years?

7 a) A shop makes a profit of 35% on all goods it sells. If it sells a sofa for £875 find the cost price of the sofa. How much profit does the shop make, to the nearest £?

b) The shop then decides to make £300 profit on selling the same model of sofa. What percentage profit does the shop now make? Give your answer to 1 d.p.

Revision Unit 4

Ratio, conversions and compound measure

The Check Up

1 a) Write the ratio 5 : 7 in the form 1 : *n*. ______

b) Fin contributes £5, Rob £3 and Mark £2 to buy a lottery ticket which wins £750. How much do they each win if they share their winning in proportion to their contributions? ______

c) The real distance between A and B is 5 km. Find the scale of this map.

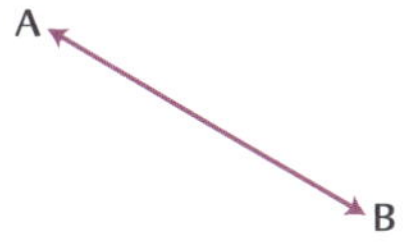

______

d) On a map with scale 1 : 25 000 Chis and Worth are 6 cm apart. How far are they apart in real life? Give your answer in kilometres. ______

2 a) The distance between Paris and Clara's home is 300 km.

Approximately how far is this in miles? ______

b) At the supermarket, 2 kg of apples cost £3.60.

What is the approximate price per pound? ______

c) Peter buys 2 litres of milk.

Approximately how many pints has he bought? ______

3 a) A recipe to make 18 buns needs 150 g of flour.

How many grams of flour are needed to make 12 buns? ______

b) £1 is worth 1.52 euros. How much is £47.50 worth in euros? ______

c) How much is \$60 worth in pounds if the exchange rate is £1 to \$1.70? ______

d) Ralph discovers that 750 g of lawn feed covers an area of 12 m^2.

How much fertiliser will he need for an area of 22 m^2? ______

e) A school plans to buy 300 text books which cost £12.50 each. A reduction of £2.00 is allowed on each book.

How many books can the school now buy for the same money? ______

4 Convert 20 m/s into km/h. ______

Mark yourself *(see answers on page 99)*

- Just a few wrong? You're geared up for the Exam Practice Questions. Go for it!
- More than a few wrong? Boost your learning powers by taking the Crash Course before you tackle the Exam Practice Questions.

/ 13

The Crash Course

Ratio

Ratios are used to compare amounts. If two sisters are 4 years old and 7 years old then the ratio of their ages is 4 compared to 7. This can be written as 4 : 7 (say 4 to 7).

Ratios in different forms

Ratios work in the same way as fractions. If you multiply or divide one side of the ratio, you must do the same to the other side.

$4:7 = 40:70$ (Multiply both parts of the ratio by 10.) Compare this with the fractions: $\frac{4}{7} = \frac{40}{70}$

It can be useful to write a ratio in the form $1:n$.

To write the ratio 4 : 7 in the form $1:n$, divide both sides by 4. So $4:7 = 1:\frac{7}{4} = 1:1.75$.

Steps for dividing an amount in a given ratio

Mel earns £216 a week and spends it on partying, necessities and travel in the ratio 3 : 7 : 2.
How much does she spend on partying and how much on travel?

1. Add the ratios together. $3 + 7 + 2 = 12$
2. Divide the amount by 12 to get one part. One part is $£216 \div 12 = £18$
3. Work out three and two parts. Partying: three parts is $£18 \times 3 = £54$ Travel: two parts is $£18 \times 2 = £36$
   She spends £54 on partying and £36 on travel.

Map scales

A map is a scaled-down representation of a large area. A scale of 1 : 50 000 means 1 unit on the map represents 50 000 of the same units on the ground. So 1 cm on the map represents 50 000 cm = 500 m = 0.5 km on the ground.

How to work out a real distance from a map

On Dave's map the scale is 1 : 50 000 and two schools are 3 cm apart. Find their real distance apart in kilometres.
In real life a 3 cm map measurement is $3 \text{ cm} \times 50\,000 = 150\,000 \text{ cm}$
Convert 150 000 cm to km:
$1 \text{ km} = 100\,000 \text{ cm}$ so $150\,000 \text{ cm} = 150\,000 \div 100\,000 \text{ km} = 1.5 \text{ km}$
The schools are 1.5 km apart.

Tip: 50 000 is the scale factor of the map.

How to work out map distances

In real life two sports centres are 8 km apart. How far apart would they be on Dave's map?
Reverse the steps. First convert km to cm: $8 \text{ km} = 8 \times 100\,000 \text{ cm} = 800\,000 \text{ cm}$
On the map 800 000 cm is represented by $800\,000 \text{ cm} \div 50\,000 = 16 \text{ cm}$ (1 d.p.)
The sports centres are 16 cm apart on the map.

How to work out a map scale

Measure as accurately as possible the distance between two points on the map and compare it with the real distance between the same two points.

Example

On a map two sports shops are 5.5 cm apart, following the road. The real distance is 2.2 km. What is the map's scale?
The scale is 5.5 cm : 2.2 km = 5.5 : 220 000 Work in the same units.

$$= 1 : \frac{220\,000}{5.5} = 1 : 40\,000$$ Divide both sides by 5.5.

The map scale is 1 : 40 000.

Key facts and skills

- ratios are used to compare quantities
- ratios behave like fractions, and can be reduced to simplest terms
- ratios can be written in different forms including $1:n$
- amounts can be divided in a given ratio
- to change a map measurement to a real distance multiply by the map scale factor
- to change a ground distance to a map measurement divide by the map scale factor

THE CRASH COURSE

Conversions

How to convert quantities for different situations

Think when to divide and when to multiply. If you want more then you multiply. If you want less you divide.

EXAMPLES

- These are the ingredients for making 18 flapjacks.
  How much do you need for 6 flapjacks?
  To make 6 flapjacks you need less so divide. 18 ÷ 6 = 3 so divide the quantities by 3.
  You need 6 oz ÷ 3 = 2 oz margarine
  8 oz ÷ 3 = $\frac{2}{3}$ oz brown sugar
  12 oz ÷ 3 = 4 oz rolled oats.

  6 oz margarine
  8 oz brown sugar
  12 oz rolled oats
- Gwen provided enough food for 5 campers for 7 days. It rained so only 3 campers arrived. How long would you expect the food to last?
  There is enough food for 5 campers.
  The same amount of food will last 1 camper more days so multiply.
  If 5 campers have food for 7 days 1 camper has food for 7 × 5 = 35 days.
  Now to feed 3 campers the food will last fewer (less) days so divide.
  Then 3 campers have food for 35 ÷ 3 = 11.667 days (3 d.p.)
  There is enough food to last 3 campers approximately 11 days.

How to use estimates to convert from one system of units to another

Learn the following conversion factors. The symbol ≈ means 'is approximately equal to'.

1 kg ≈ 2.2 lbs	8 km ≈ 5 miles
1 litre ≈ 1.75 pints	1 metre ≈ 39 inches
1 gallon ≈ 4.5 litres	30 cm ≈ 1 foot

EXAMPLE

Who has walked further, Jane who walks 15 miles or Jaques who walks 20 km?
1 mile is approximately 8 ÷ 5 km.
Jane walks 15 miles which is approximately 8 ÷ 5 × 15 km = 24 km. So Jane has walked further.

Foreign currency

To help convert money between currencies, banks work out tables of **exchange rates** which tell customers what they will get for their money.

EXAMPLES

Use the exchange rate £1 = $1.61 to convert between pounds and dollars.

- How many dollars would you expect to get for £200?
  £1 = $1.61 → you will get more dollars for each pound so multiply. £200 = 200 × $1.61 = $322
- You have $60. How much should this be worth in pounds?
  Use the exchange rate $1.61 = £1
  You will get less pounds for each dollar so divide. $60 = 60 ÷ £1.61 = £37.27 (2 d.p.)

KEY FACTS AND SKILLS

For conversions:

- if you want **more** then **multiply**
- if you want **less** then **divide**
- use **exchange rates** or **conversion factors** to change from one system of units to another

THE CRASH COURSE

Compound measures

Density, speed and the cost of fabric per metre are examples of compound measures.

Density

This is the mass (weight) of one unit of volume of the substance.
Think of the weight of a box filled with feathers and the weight of the same box filled with lead. The box with lead is heavier. Lead has a greater density than feathers.
These are the formulae connecting density (D), mass (M) and volume (V).

$D = \frac{M}{V}$ $V = \frac{M}{D}$ $M = D \times V$ Use this triangle to help you remember.

EXAMPLE

The density of milk is 0.98 g/cm^3. What is the mass (weight) of half a litre of milk?
$V = 0.5$ litres $= 500$ cm^3 (Work in same units and remember that 1 litre = 1000 cm^3.)
$D = 0.98$ g/cm^3
Mass of milk, $M = D \times V = 0.98 \times 500 = 490$ g

Speed

For a problem involving speed, use the distance (D), speed (S), time (T) triangle.

$S = \frac{D}{T}$ $T = \frac{D}{S}$ $D = S \times T$

Average speed

To find an average speed, work with the total distance and total time.

EXAMPLE

A car travels at 45 mph for 2 hours. It stops for 30 minutes, and then continues at a steady speed of 65 mph along the motorway for 2 hour 45 minutes. Find the car's average speed over the whole journey.
Total time is $2 + 0.5 + 2.75$ hours $= 5.25$ hours
Distance for first part of journey is $45 \times 2 = 90$ miles (mph × h = miles)
Distance for second part of journey is $65 \times 2.75 = 178.75$ miles
Total distance is $90 + 178.75$ miles $= 268.75$ miles
Average speed $= \frac{\text{total distance}}{\text{total time}} = \frac{268.75}{5.25}$ mph $= 51.1904\ldots$ mph $= 51.2$ mph (1 d.p.)

Tip:
Take care with times.
Remember that 0.4 hours is 24 minutes, not 40 minutes.

Converting units of speed

To convert speed to different units, think very carefully when to divide and when to multiply.

EXAMPLE

Convert a speed of 50 kilometres per hour to metres per second.
50 km/h $= 50 \times 1000$ metre/h $= 50\,000$ metre/h (To convert km to m multiply by 1000.)
$= 50\,000 \div 60 \div 60$ m/s (To convert seconds to hours divide because you go less far in 1 second than in 1 hour.)
$= 13.8.$ m/s

Tip: For problems involving compound measure (look out for 'per') take care and make sure you know when to divide and when to multiply.

KEY FACTS AND SKILLS

- for density: $M = D \times V$, $D = M \div V$, $V = M \div D$
- for speed: $D = S \times T$, $S = D \div T$, $T = D \div S$
- in compound measures 'per' means divide

Exam Practice Questions

1 a) In Claire's bag of pick 'n' mix sweets the ratio of fruit drops to humbugs is 5 : 7. If there are 60 sweets in the bag how many are fruit drops?

b) In Rob's bag of sweets the ratio of mints to toffees is 5 : 4. If there are 20 toffees how many sweets are there altogether?

c) Rob changes his mind. He keeps the total number of sweets the same, but increases the number of toffees so that there are twice as many toffees as mints. How many extra toffees will there be in the bag?

2 Which is the best value for money? Explain your answer.

3 A plan has the scale of 2 cm to 1 m.

a) Write this in the form 1 : *n*.

b) On the plan the base of a patio door is 5.5 cm. How wide is the real patio door?

c) A door is 75 cm wide. What width would this be on the plan?

4 In France Charles cashes a £50 travellers' cheque. He is charged commission of 10 francs. The exchange rate is £1.00 = 9.64 francs.

a) How many francs does he get?

b) He then buys 1 kg of grapes which costs him 18 francs. Assuming the same exchange rate, approximately how much do the grapes cost in £?

c) What is the approximate price of 1 lb of grapes in £?

5 What is the average speed of the journey shown on the graph?

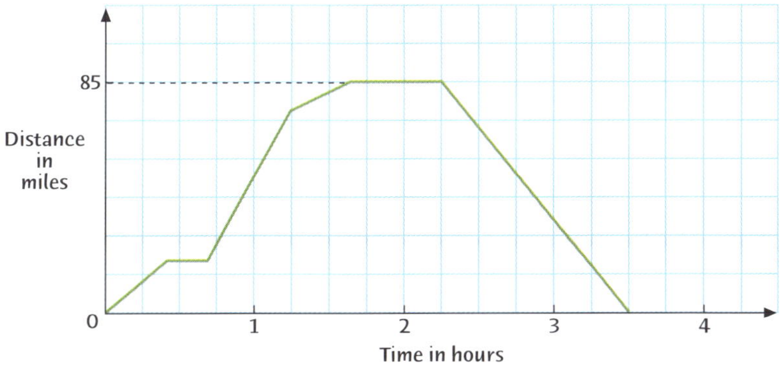

6 Pila bought 4.5 m of fabric costing £2.39 per metre. She made a mistake and really wanted 4.5 yards. (36 inches = 1 yard)

a) How much extra fabric did she buy?

b) How much money has she wasted?

Revision Unit 5

Algebra

The Check Up

1 Simplify these expressions.

a) $2a + 3ab - 5a + ba - b$ __________

b) $2x^2 + 3xy - y^2 + 2xy - 3y^2$ __________

c) $a^2 \times a^4$ __________

d) $5p^4 \times 3p^2$ __________

e) $10x^3 \div 2x$ __________

f) $(4x^3)^3$ __________

2 Expand and simplify these expressions.

a) $4y(2y + 3)$ __________

b) $-x(4x - 2)$ __________

c) $(x + 2)(x + 5)$ __________

d) $(2b - 3)(3b + 1)$ __________

e) $(3a + 5)^2$ __________

3 Simplify these expressions.

a) $3a + 5a(a - 1)$ __________

b) $2x^2 - 3x(x - 5)$ __________

c) $9 - (2x + 4)$ __________

4 When a ball is thrown vertically upward the maximum height it reaches, h in m, is given by $h = \frac{u^2}{2g}$ when u m/s is the speed with which the ball is thrown.
Calculate h when the ball is thrown with a speed of 20 m/s and $g = 9.81$ m/s^2. __________

5 The formula to change a temperature in degrees Celsius, C, into a temperature in degrees Fahrenheit, F, is:

$$F = 1.8C + 32$$

What is a temperature of 8°C in degrees Fahrenheit? __________

If the temperature is 85°F what is this in degrees Celsius? __________

Mark yourself *(see answers on page 99)*

- Just a few wrong? You're geared up for the Exam Practice Questions. Go for it!
- More than a few wrong? Boost your learning powers by taking the Crash Course before you tackle the Exam Practice Questions.

/ 17

THE CRASH COURSE

Substitution

In algebra, letters are used to stand for numbers. Because the letters stand for numbers, they can be added, subtracted, multiplied and divided, just like numbers. Any letter can be used, although x and y are used most commonly.
Substitution means replacing the letters in an expression with numbers. When substituting, take care with negative signs. Sometimes it helps to put brackets round the numbers that are being substituted.

How to add and subtract with negative numbers

Add a negative number like this: $7 + (-3) = 7 - 3 = 4$
Subtract a negative number like this: $7 - (-3) = 7 + 3 = 10$

Tip: If there is no sign in front of a number, it is positive.

EXAMPLES

Work out the value of $x + y$ and $x - y$ when $x = 12$ and $y = -5$.

- $x + y = (12) + (-5) = 12 - 5 = 7$
- $x - y = (12) - (-5) = 12 + 5 = 17$

How to multiply and divide with negative numbers

Multiplying or dividing two numbers with the **same** sign (both positive or both negative) gives a **positive** answer.

$(12) \div (3) = 4$ $\quad (-12) \div (-3) = 4$ $\quad (12) \times (3) = 36$ $\quad (-12) \times (-3) = 36$

Multiplying or dividing two numbers with **different** signs (one is positive and the other is negative) gives a **negative** answer.

$(12) \div (-3) = -4$ $\quad (-12) \div (3) = -4$ $\quad (-12) \times (3) = -36$ $\quad (12) \times (-3) = -36$

EXAMPLES

- Work out the value of $a \times b$ when $a = -18$ and $b = 2$.
  $a \times b = (-18) \times (2) = -36$
- Work out the value of $a \div b$ when $a = -18$ and $b = -2$.
  $a \div b = (-18) \div (-2) = 9$

How to substitute numbers into formulae

$s = ut + 0.5at^2$ is a formula which gives the distance s travelled in time t, for an object that started with velocity u and moved with constant acceleration a. Find the value for s when $a = -10$, $t = 6$ and $u = 30.4$.

$s = (30.4) \times (6) + 0.5 \times (-10) \times (6^2) = 182.4 + (-180) = 2.4$

Terms and expressions

A **term** may be made up of numbers, letters or a mixture of both.
An **expression** is a group of terms. $4y^2 - y + 3$ is an expression.
$4y^2$ is the y^2-term and is positive. (It has an invisible + sign in front of it.)
$4y^2$ means $4 \times y \times y$.
$-y$ is the y-term and is negative. It has a − sign in front of it. No number has been written in front of it, but $-y$ really means $-1 \times y$.
$+3$ is the number term and has a + sign.

Tip: In algebra, write $7 \times y$ as $7y$ and $1 \times y$ as just y.

THE CRASH COURSE

How to simplify an expression

An expression may be simplified by adding, subtracting, multiplying and dividing terms.

How to simplify by adding and subtracting

Only **like terms** can be added or subtracted to make one new term.
Add or subtract all the y-terms or all the x-terms or all the y^2-terms, but don't try to add or subtract an x-term to a y-term.

EXAMPLES

- $y + 5y = 6y$ — There are two y-terms so you can add them together.
- $y^2 - 4y^2 = -3y^2$ — There are two y^2-terms so you can subtract.
- $xy + 4yx = 5xy$ or $5yx$ — There are two like terms ($xy = yx$) so you can add them.
- $7y^3 + 2y^2$ — y^3 and y^2 are not like terms so you cannot add them.

How to simplify by multiplying

First multiply the numbers, then multiply the letters.

EXAMPLES

- $y \times y \times y = y^3$ — Compare this with how $4 \times 4 \times 4$ can be written as 4^3.
- $3y \times 5y = 3 \times 5 \times y \times y = 15 \times y \times y$ — Multiply 3 by 5.
  $= 15 \times y^2 = 15y^2$ — Now multiply the letters.
- $2ab \times 9bc = 2 \times 9 \times a \times b \times b \times c = 18 \times a \times b \times b \times c$ — Multiply 2 by 9.
  $= 18ab^2c$ — Now multiply the letters.

Tip: Writing the letters in alphabetical order makes it easier to keep track of them.

How to simplify expressions with indices

x^3 means multiply $x \times x \times x$. Say 'x to the power of three' or 'x cubed'. The 3 is called the index.
As before, multiply (or divide) the numbers and then multiply (or divide) the letters. Use the rules of indices when multiplying or dividing powers.

The rules of indices

Multiplying powers

- $y^3 \times y^2 = y \times y \times y \times y \times y = y^5$

To multiply powers of the **same** letter, **add** the indices:

$y^3 \times y^2 = y^{(3+2)} = y^5$

- $7a^4 \times 3a^5 = 7 \times 3 \times a^4 \times a^5 = 21 \times a^4 \times a^5$ — Multiply 7 by 3.
  $= 21a^{(4+5)} = 21a^9$ — Now multiply the letters.

Tip: $3a^2$ means $3 \times a \times a$ but $(3a)^2$ means $3 \times a \times 3 \times a = 3^2 \times a^2 = 9a^2$

Dividing powers

- $y^5 \div y^2 = \frac{y \times y \times y \times \not{y} \times \not{y}}{\not{y} \times \not{y}} = y^3$

To divide powers of the **same** letter, **subtract** the indices.

$y^5 \div y^2 = y^{(5-2)} = y^3$

- $8a^6 \div 2a^5 = \frac{8}{2}(a^6 \div a^5) = 4(a^6 \div a^5)$ — Divide 8 by 2.
  $= 4a^{(6-5)} = 4a^1 = 4a$ — Now divide the letters.

Raising powers to a power

- $(x^2)^3 = x^2 \times x^2 \times x^2 = x^6$

To raise a power to a power, **multiply** the indices.

$(x^2)^3 = x^{2 \times 3} = x^6$

- $(3x^2)^2 = 3^2 \times (x^2)^2 = 9(x^2)^2$ — Multiply 3 by 3.
  $= 9x^{(2 \times 2)} = 9x^4$ — Raise the power to the power 2.

The Crash Course

Brackets

Brackets are used to group terms that must all be multiplied by another number or letter. **Expanding** the brackets means getting rid of the brackets by multiplying out.

Expressions with one bracket

To multiply an expression with one bracket, multiply everything inside the bracket by the number (or letter) outside the bracket.

- $4(y + 3)$ means $4 \times y + 4 \times 3$ Multiply the y and the +3 inside the bracket by 4.
  $4(y + 3) = 4y + 12$
- $-2y(y + 5)$ means $-2y \times y + -2y \times +5$
  $-2y(y + 5) = -2y^2 - 10y$ Multiply the y and the +5 inside the bracket by −2y.
- $-(2x + 7) = -2x - 7$ Multiply the 2x and the +7 inside the bracket by −1.

Expressions with two brackets

To multiply an expression which is the product of two brackets, everything in the second bracket must be multiplied by everything in the first bracket.

$(2x + 3)(x - 4)$ means $(2x + 3) \times (x - 4)$.

Multiply $(x - 4)$ by $2x$ **and** multiply $(x - 4)$ by $+3$.

Multiply the terms in this order: $(2x + 3)(x - 4) =$ (O, F, I, L)

First is	Outer is	Inner is	Last is
$2x \times x$	$2x \times -4$	$+3 \times x$	$+3 \times -4$
$= 2x^2$	$= -8x$	$= +3x$	$= -12$

So $(2x + 3)(x - 4) = 2x^2 - 8x + 3x - 12$

Now to simplify, subtract like x-terms: $-8x + 3x = -5x$

$(2x + 3)(x - 4) = 2x^2 - 8x + 3x - 12 = 2x^2 - 5x - 12$

Tip:
Learn FOIL
First Outer Inner Last

Example

- Expand the brackets and simplify $(B + b)(B + 5b)$.

$(B + b)(B + 5b) =$

First is	Outer is	Inner is	Last is
$B \times B$	$B \times +5b$	$+b \times B$	$+b \times +5b$
$= B^2$	$= +5Bb$	$= +bB$	$= 5b^2$

Do not be confused as B and b stand for different numbers so they are not like terms.

$(B + b)(B + 5b) = B^2 + 5Bb + bB + 5b^2$

Now to simplify, add like bB (or Bb) terms: $+5Bb + bB = 6Bb$

$(B + b)(B + 5b) = B^2 + 5Bb + bB + 5b^2 = B^2 + 6Bb + 5b^2$

Tip:
$(3x - 5)^2$ means $(3x - 5)(3x - 5)$

Key Facts and Skills

- use brackets when **substituting numbers for letters**
- take care with signs when **substituting negative numbers**
- only **like terms** can be added and subtracted
- to **multiply** terms, first multiply the numbers then multiply the letters
- to **multiply** terms that are **powers of the same letter add** the indices
- to **divide** terms cancel the numbers and then the letters
- to **divide** terms that are **powers of the same letter subtract** the indices
- to **multiply using one bracket** multiply each term inside the bracket by the term outside
- to **multiply using two brackets** remember **FOIL**

EXAM PRACTICE QUESTIONS

1 Simplify this expression.
$3x - 2xy + 7y + 4x + yx$

2 Expand and simplify this expression.
$(3x - 2)(x + 5)$

3 Expand this expression. Write your answer as simply as possible.
$(A + a)(A - a)$

4 The lengths of the sides of a triangle are $(y + 2)$ cm, $(y + 3)$ cm and $(y - 1)$ cm, as shown.
Write an expression in terms of y for the perimeter of the triangle.
Give your answer in its simplest form.

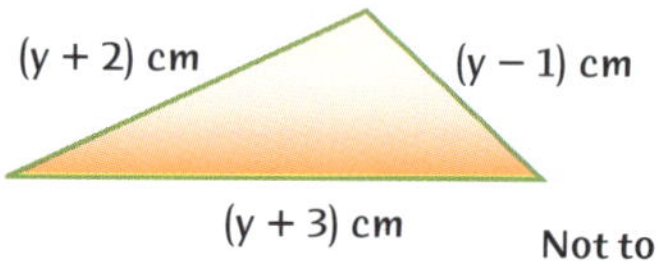

Not to scale

5 Write down the areas of these two rectangles in the simplest form.

a)

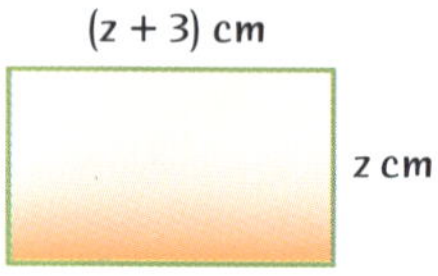

b)

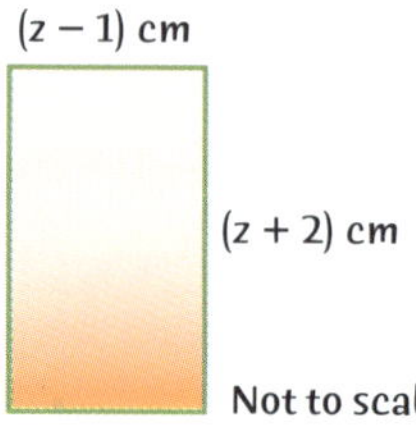

Not to scale

6 Show that $(a + 1)^2 - 2(a - 1) - 3 = a^2$

7 Simplify these expressions.
a) $6y^5 \div 3y^2$
b) $4x^3 \times 2x^5$
c) $(4y^2)^3$

8 This is a formula for the starting velocity u in m/s: $u = \sqrt{v^2 - 2as}$.
Find the value of u when $v = 12$ m/s, $a = -9.8$ m/s^2, $s = 38$ m.
Check your answer using numbers correct to 1 s.f.

9 A number e which determines how a ball bounces is given by $e = \dfrac{V - v}{U - u}$.
Find e when: $V = 7.89$, $v = 1.93$, $U = 6.68$ and $u = -3.25$.
Check your answer using numbers correct to 1 s.f.

Revision Unit 6

Linear equations and formulae

The Check Up

1 Solve the following equations.

a) $3x + 4 = 13$ ______________

b) $\frac{2}{5}x = 8$ ______________

c) $2(3z + 1) = 26$ ______________

d) $5y + 4 = 7y - 6$ ______________

e) $3(b - 4) = 2 + b$ ______________

f) $\frac{5}{2}x - 9 = 1$ ______________

2 a) You are given the formula $C = 5 + 3N$.

Make N the subject of the formula. ______________

b) You are given the formula $V = ab^2$.

Make b the subject of the formula. ______________

c) You are given the formula $P = a + \pi r$.

Rearrange the formula to make r the subject. ______________

3 Solve the following inequalities.

a) $4 + 5a < 14$ ______________

b) $3b - 4 > 2b - 5$ ______________

c) $2(x - 4) \leqslant 12$ ______________

d) $-4 \leqslant 3a + 2 < 11$ ______________

Mark yourself *(see answers on page 100)*

- Just a few wrong? You're geared up for the Exam Practice Questions. Go for it!
- More than a few wrong? Boost your learning powers by taking the Crash Course before you tackle the Exam Practice Questions.

/13

THE CRASH COURSE

Linear equations

Linear equations have one unknown, or letter.
$4x + 6 = 50$ and $9x + 8 = 7x - 3$ are linear equations.
The unknown in this equation is x.

Tip:
Unknowns are also called variables.

Making equations

Sometimes problems can be solved by making an equation. Although x is often used for the unknown number, any other letter could be used.

EXAMPLE

The sum of four consecutive whole numbers is 50. Make an equation to find the first number.
Use x for the first number. The next number is one more which is $(x + 1)$.
The next number is two more which is $(x + 2)$ and the last number is $(x + 3)$.
So the equation is $x + (x + 1) + (x + 2) + (x + 3) = 50$
Add the x-terms and add the number terms. The equation is $4x + 6 = 50$.

Three rules for solving linear equations

To solve a linear equation, find the value of the unknown letter.

1 **What is done to one side must also be done to the other**

The equation is like a balance. Anything added to one side must also be added to the other side. Aim to get the letter term by itself.

EXAMPLES

- Solve the equation $4x + 6 = 50$.
  To get rid of the '+6' subtract 6 from each side: $4x + 6 - 6 = 50 - 6$
  $4x = 44$
  To get rid of the 'multiply by 4' divide each side by 4: $4x \div 4 = 44 \div 4$
  $x = 11$
- Solve $\frac{3b}{2} = 9$.
  To get rid of the 'divide by 2' multiply both sides by 2: $3b = 9 \times 2 = 18$
  To get rid of the 'multiply by 3' divide each side by 3: $b = 18 \div 3 = 6$

2 **Collect all the letter terms on one side and the number terms on the other**

EXAMPLE

Solve the equation $9x + 8 = 7x - 3$.
To get all the x-terms on one side subtract $7x$ from both sides: $9x - 7x + 8 = 7x - 7x - 3$
$2x + 8 = -3$
Now to get the x-term by itself subtract 8 from both sides: $2x + 8 - 8 = -3 - 8$
$2x = -11$
To get rid of the 'multiply by 2' divide both sides by 2: $y = -11 \div 2 = -5\frac{1}{2}$ or -5.5

3 **Get rid of any brackets**

EXAMPLE

Solve the equation $2(x + 5) = 5(x - 1)$.
Get rid of the brackets: $2x + 10 = 5x - 5$
To get all the x-terms on one side subtract $2x$ from both sides: $2x - 2x + 10 = 5x - 2x - 5$
$10 = 3x - 5$
To get the x-term by itself add 5 to both sides: $10 + 5 = 3x - 5 + 5$
$15 = 3x$
To get rid of the 'multiply by 3' divide both sides by 3: $5 = x$

Tip:
It is easier to put the x-terms on the side which keeps them positive.

The Crash Course

How to transform or change the subject of a formula

Rearrange the formula so that the required letter is on its own on one side. Use the rules of linear equations.

Example

Make t the subject of this formula: $v = u + gt$.

Circle the term with the required letter: $v = u + \boxed{gt}$

To get this term by itself, subtract u from both sides: $v - u = u - u + gt$

$v - u = gt$

To get rid of the 'multiply by g', divide both sides by g: $\dfrac{v - u}{g} = t$

Formulae with squares or square roots

First get the square or square root term by itself. If it is a square, get rid of it by taking square roots on each side. If it is a square root, get rid of it by squaring each side.

Example

Find the surface area, A, of a sphere given that the radius $r = \sqrt{\dfrac{A}{4\pi}}$.

To get rid of the square root, square each side: $r^2 = \dfrac{A}{4\pi}$

To get rid of the 'divide by 4π, multiply both sides by 4π: $4\pi r^2 = A$ or, writing A first, $A = 4\pi r^2$.

How to solve linear inequalities

Use the same rules as for solving linear equations except that multiplying or dividing by a negative number changes the direction of the inequality.

For example: 3 is greater than 1 $3 > 1$

Multiply both sides by -1 and **change the direction of the inequality**. $-3 < -1$

> **Tip:**
> Avoid confusion by collecting the required term on the side which keeps it positive.

Examples

- Solve $19 - 2x > 9$.
  Add $2x$ to each side, to make the x-term positive: $19 - 2x + 2x > 2x + 9$
  Subtract 9 from each side: $19 - 9 > 2x$
  $10 > 2x$
  Divide each side by 2: $5 > x$ or, writing x first, $x < 5$
- Solve $-1 < x + 4 < 6$.
  Adapt the rules and it's not as difficult as it looks.
  Make sure that whatever is done to one side is done to the middle and the other side.
  To get x by itself subtract 4 from each side and the middle: $-1 - 4 < x < 6 - 4$
  $-5 < x < 2$

Key facts and skills

- to **solve linear equations**, get the unknown term by itself
- what is done to **one side** must be done to **the other**
- if there are any **brackets**, get rid of them by multiplying
- collect **letter terms on one side** and **number terms on the other**
- **transform the subject of a formula** by using the rules of linear equations
- to make a **squared term** the subject isolate it, then take the square root on each side
- to make a **square root term** the subject isolate it then square both sides
- solve **inequalities** by treating them like linear equations **but** collect letter terms on the side which makes them positive

EXAM PRACTICE QUESTIONS

1 Yummy bars cost 70p each and Scrummy bars cost 60p each.

a) Jon buys x yummy bars.
Write down an expression in terms of x, for the cost of Jon's bars.

b) Abby buys p yummy bars and q scrummy bars.
Write down an expression, in terms of p and q, for the total cost of Abby's bars.

c) The cost of r yummy bars and 3 scrummy bars is £4.60.
Write this as an equation in terms of r.

d) Use your equation to find the value of r.

2 A rectangle has a length of $(x + 7)$ cm and a width of $(x - 3)$ cm.
If the perimeter of the rectangle is 30 cm, what is the value of x?

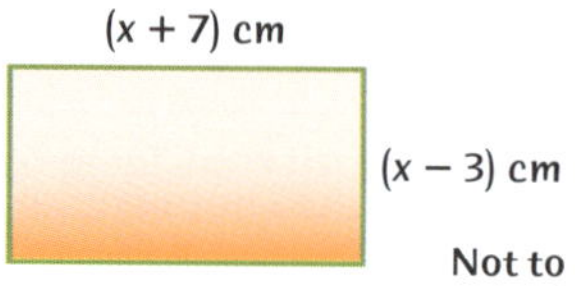

Not to scale

3 Solve these equations.

a) $\frac{9}{2}x = 36$

b) $4y + 9 = 23$

c) $3z + 6 = 22 - z$

4 Solve the equation $3(4x + 1) = 21$.

5 Solve this equation.

$$7 + \frac{3x}{2} = 16$$

6 Solve the following inequalities for x.

a) $1 + 5x < 21$

b) $5x - 7 > 4x - 2$

7 Solve this inequality.

$$-2 \leqslant 3x + 4 < 5$$

8 This is the formula to find the cost C of giving a party for P people.
$C = 65 + 7.5P$
Make P the subject of the formula.

9 You are given the formula $V = \frac{1}{3}xy^2$.

a) Find the value of V when $x = 4.15 \times 10^5$ and $y = 0.7$.
Give your answer in standard form to 2 d.p.

b) Rearrange the formula $V = \frac{1}{3}xy^2$ to give y in terms of V and x.

Revision Unit 1

Factorising and quadratics

The Check Up

1 Factorise these expressions completely.

a) $120a + 40$ ____________

b) $5x^3 - x$ ____________

c) $10x^2 + 6x$ ____________

d) $9pq^3 - 12p^3q^2$ ____________

2 Factorise these expressions.

a) $x^2 + 5x + 6$ ____________

b) $x^2 + 3x - 10$ ____________

c) $a^2 - 7a - 18$ ____________

d) $A^2 - 9A + 20$ ____________

3 Solve these equations.

a) $x^2 - 10x - 24 = 0$ ____________

b) $q^2 + 2q = 15$ ____________

c) $3y^2 - 9y = 0$ ____________

4 Solve these.

a) $x^2 = 49$ ____________

b) $x^2 \leqslant 4$ ____________

Mark yourself *(see answers on page 100)*

- Just a few wrong? You're geared up for the Exam Practice Questions. Go for it!
- More than a few wrong? Boost your learning powers by taking the Crash Course before you tackle the Exam Practice Questions.

/13

THE CRASH COURSE

Factorising

Factorising means taking factors out of an expression, and putting brackets back into it.
There are two different types of expression that can be factorised.
The first type can be factorised using one set of brackets and the second type can be factorised using two sets of brackets.

Factorising using one set of brackets

Look at the expression to be factorised, to find the common factor.

EXAMPLES

- Factorise $2x + 6$.
  Write $2x$ as $2 \times x$ and 6 as 2×3: $2x + 6 = 2 \times x + 2 \times 3$
  Circle the common factor 2: $2x + 6 = \textcircled{2} \times x + \textcircled{2} \times 3$
  Take out the common factor 2, leaving $(x + 3)$: $2x + 6 = 2(x + 3)$
  Check: $2(x + 3) = 2x + 6$ ✓
- Factorise $8x^2 + 20x$.
  Write $8x^2$ as $2 \times 2 \times 2 \times x \times x$ and $20x$ as $2 \times 2 \times 5 \times x$: $8x^2 + 20x = 2 \times 2 \times 2 \times x \times x + 2 \times 2 \times 5 \times x$
  Circle the common factors: $8x^2 + 20x = 2 \times (2 \times 2 \times x) \times x + (2 \times 2) \times 5 (\times x)$
  Take out the common factor $2 \times 2 \times x$ which is $4x$, leaving $(2x + 5)$: $8x^2 + 20x = 4x(2x + 5)$
  Check: $4x(2x + 5) = 8x^2 + 20x$ ✓

Tip: Always check inside the bracket to make sure you have all the common factors.

Factorising using two sets of brackets

Expressions like $x^2 + 5x + 6$ are **quadratic expressions**. They can often be factorised using two sets of brackets.

Steps for factorising using two sets of brackets

1 Write the expression using two sets of brackets: $x^2 + 5x + 6 = (x + \square)(x + \square)$
2 Look at the factor pairs of the number term.
The number term is +6 so the factor pairs of +6 are +6, +1 and +3, +2.
3 To find the numbers to go in the boxes, choose the factor pair that adds up to the number in front of the x-term.
Choose the factor pair +3, +2 because +2 + +3 = +5, the number in front of the x-term.
So $x^2 + 5x + 6 = (x + 2)(x + 3)$

EXAMPLE

Factorise $x^2 - 4x - 12$.
1 Write the expression using two sets of brackets: $x^2 - 4x - 12 = (x + \square)(x + \square)$
2 Look at the factor pairs of −12.
Look for factor pairs with different signs, to give negative 12.
The factor pair must add to give a −4 so the larger number must be negative.
The factor pairs of −12 to look at are: −12, +1 −6, +2 −4, +3
3 Choose the factor pair −6, +2 which adds to give −4.
So $x^2 - 2x - 24 = (x - 6)(x + 4)$.

The Crash Course

Quadratic equations

A quadratic equation must have a squared term.
Two examples of quadratic equations are $x^2 + 3x - 4 = 0$ and $3x^2 + 2x = 0$.
These examples have x^2-terms.

Making a quadratic equation

Many mathematical problems can be solved by using quadratic equations.

Example

A rectangular plot of land has an area of 12 m^2. The length of the plot is 4 m more than the width. Make an equation using the given information.
Let the length of the plot be x metres. Then the width is $(x - 4)$ metres.
The area is length times width $= x \times (x - 4)$ square metres (m^2).
The area is 12 m^2 so $x \times (x - 4) = 12$.
Work out the brackets. The equation is $x^2 - 4x = 12$.

Solving a quadratic equation

A quadratic equation can be solved by factorising or by drawing a graph.

Steps for solving a quadratic equation by factorising

Solve $x^2 - 4x = 12$.

1 Put all the terms on one side, leaving 0 on the other side. $x^2 - 4x - 12 = 0$
Write the x^2-term first, then the x-term and finally the number.
2 Factorise, following this order.
a) Look for a common factor (in this case none).
b) Follow the steps for factorising a quadratic expression.
$x^2 - 4x - 12 = (x - 6)(x + 2)$
3 If two numbers multiplied together give 0, then one or both of the numbers must equal 0.
The equation is $(x - 6) \times (x + 2) = 0$ so this means $(x - 6) = 0$ or $(x + 2) = 0$.
The solution is $x = 6$ or $x = -2$.

Tip:
Take care! Not all quadratics can be factorised in this way.

Example

Solve $3y^2 - 18y = 0$.
1 $3y^2 - 18y = 0$ This is already done in the question.
2 Factorise. Look for the common factor:
$3y^2 - 18y = (3 \times y) \times y - 2 \times 3 \times (3 \times y) = 3y(y - 6)$
3 $3y \times (y - 6) = 0$ so this means $3y = 0$ or $y - 6 = 0$.
The solution is $y = 0$ or $y = 6$.

The special easy case quadratic

To solve $x^2 = 9$, take square roots on both sides: $x = \sqrt{9} = +3$ or -3
There are **two** values because $+3 \times +3 = 9$ and $-3 \times -3 = 9$.
To solve $x^2 < 16$, take square roots on both sides, and use a number line to show the range of values.

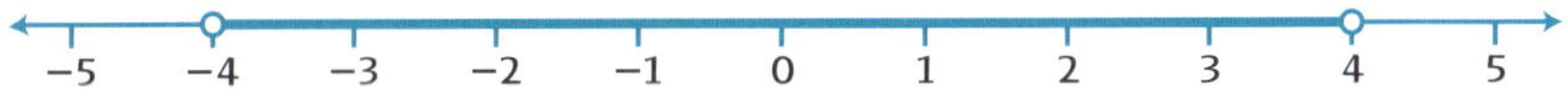

The open circle shows 4 is not included.
The solution is: $-4 < x < 4$

Tip:
If you have $\leqslant$ or $\geqslant$ then use a closed circle to show the number is included. If you have $<$ or $>$ use an open circle to show the number is not included.

Key facts and skills

- **factorise using one set of brackets** by looking for all the common factors
- **factorise many quadratic expressions** using two sets of brackets
- **solve quadratic equations** by factorising then putting each factor equal to 0
- **recognise the special case quadratics** like $x^2 = 9$ and $x^2 < 16$

Exam Practice Questions

1 Factorise completely $75A + 250$.

2 Factorise completely $7x^2 - 14x$.

3 Factorise these expressions completely.

a) $6a^2b^3 - 12a^3b^2$

b) $x^2 - 15x + 14$

4 a) Factorise the expression $x^2 + 9x + 20$.

b) Solve the equation $x^2 + 9x + 20 = 0$.

5 a) Factorise the expression $x^2 + 3x$.

b) Solve the equation $x^2 + 3x = 0$.

6 A rectangle has these dimensions.

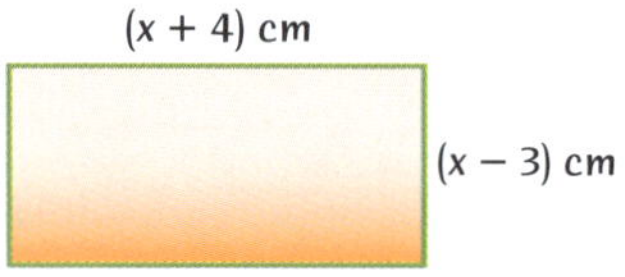

Not to scale

a) If the area of the rectangle is 144 cm², show that $x^2 + x - 156 = 0$.

b) Find the value of x when the area of the rectangle is 144 cm².

c) What are the dimensions of the rectangle?

Revision Unit 8

Plotting and using graphs

The Check Up

1 a) Make a table of values for $y = 3x - 5$ for $x = -3$, 0 and 3.

x	−3	0	3
y			

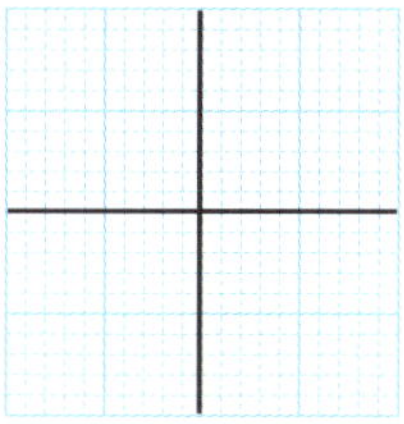

b) Plot the graph of $y = 3x - 5$.

c) From your graph find the value of x when $y = -1$. ____________

2 a) Make a table of values for $y = x^2 - 2x$ for x between −2 and +3.

x	−2	−1	0	1	2	3
y						

b) Plot the graph of $y = x^2 - 2x$.

c) By drawing the appropriate straight line solve the equation $x^2 - 2x = 1$. ____________

d) For what values of x is $x^2 - 2x < 0$? ____________

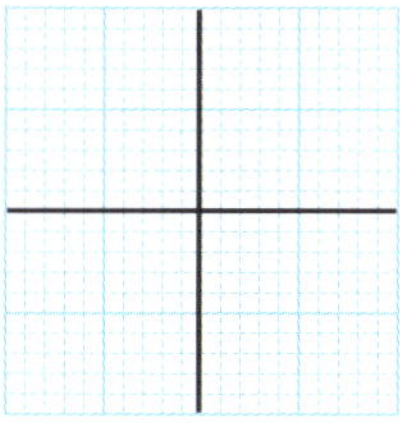

3 a) Use $x = -3$, $x = 0$ and $x = 3$ to make tables of values for $y = 2x + 4$ and for $y = 2 - x$.

x	−3	0	3
$y = 2x + 4$			
$y = 2 - x$			

b) Plot the two straight lines.

c) Read off the x- and y-coordinates of the point of intersection of the lines. ____________

d) What does this point of intersection represent? ____________

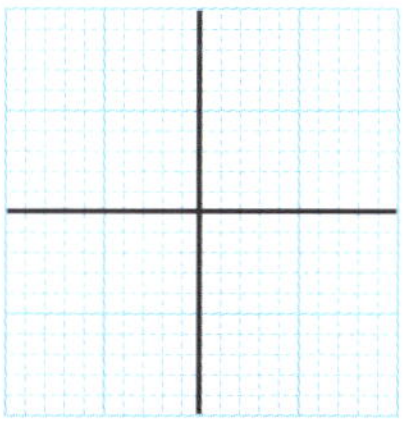

4 By plotting the appropriate straight lines show and shade the region defined by:
$x + y < 2$, $y > 1$ $x \geqslant -2$
Label the required region R.

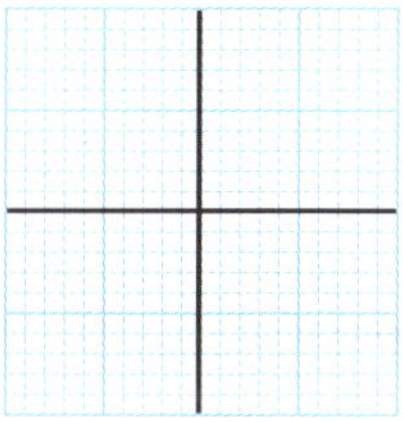

Where you see 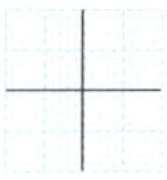 **by a question, use graph paper to draw the graphs.**

Mark yourself ***(see answers on pages 100-101)***

- Just a few wrong? You're geared up for the Exam Practice Questions. Go for it!
- More than a few wrong? Boost your learning powers by taking the Crash Course before you tackle the Exam Practice Questions.

/ 12

THE CRASH COURSE

How to plot graphs

To plot straight-line graphs, like $y = 2x + 3$, two points are enough but it's best to plot three in case of mistakes.

Graphs which are curves have terms with x^3, x^2 or $\frac{1}{x}$. They may also have a mixture of these as well as x-terms or number terms.

Steps for plotting a graph

1. Make a table of values for x and y. Be very careful with positive and negative signs when using negative x-values to calculate y.
2. Draw the x- and y-axes, choosing a suitable scale for the values to be plotted.
3. Plot corresponding x- and y-values with a sharp pencil, marking them with a clear **X**.
4. Join these points in a straight line or a smooth curve. If the curve is not smooth or the line is not straight then the values must be checked and replotted.

EXAMPLE

Plot the graph of $y = 4x^2 - 4x - 5$ for values of x between -3 and 3.

1. Make a table of values for x from -3 to 3 and calculate y.

x	-3	-2	-1	0	1	2	3
$4x^2$	$4 \times (-3)^2 = 36$	$4 \times (-2)^2 = 16$	$4 \times (-1)^2 = 4$	$4 \times (0)^2 = 0$	$4 \times (1)^2 = 4$	$4 \times (2)^2 = 16$	$4 \times (3)^2 = 36$
$-4x$	$-4 \times (-3) = 12$	$-4 \times (-2) = 8$	$-4 \times (-1) = 4$	$-4 \times (0) = 0$	$-4 \times (1) = -4$	$-4 \times (2) = -8$	$-4 \times (3) = -12$
-5	-5	-5	-5	-5	-5	-5	-5
$y = 4x^2 - 4x - 5$	43	19	3	-5	-5	3	19

2. Choose a scale for x from -3 to 3 and a scale for y from -10 to 45.
3. Plot corresponding x- and y-values e.g. $(-3, 43)$.
4. Join the points in a smooth curve to complete the graph of $y = 4x^2 - 4x - 5$.

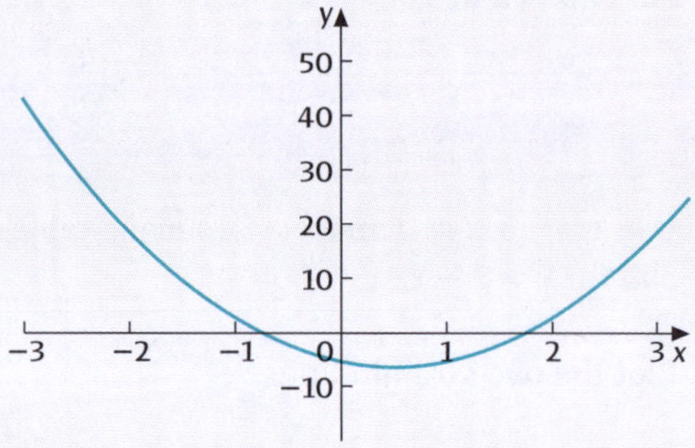

Tip:
Take care joining the curve between 0 and 1 where the y-values are both -5.
To get a smooth curve the line must dip below -5, so the minimum value of $4x^2 - 4x - 5$ is -6.

How to use graphs to solve equations

When a graph has been plotted, it can be used to solve equations.

EXAMPLE

Refer to the diagram above for this curve.

- Solve $4x^2 - 4x - 5 = 0$.
  The left-hand side of the equation, $y = 4x^2 - 4x - 5$, has already been plotted.
  The right-hand side of the equation is $y = 0$ which is the x-axis.
  The solution can be found where the curve intersects the x-axis.
  The values are $x = -0.7$ and 1.7.
- Solve $4x^2 - 4x - 5 = 15$.
  Plot the right-hand side of the equation, which is the line $y = 15$.
  The solution is where the graph and the line $y = 15$ intersect.
  Read off the required x-values to get the solution.
  The values are $x = -1.8$ and 2.8.
- Solve $4x^2 - 4x - 5 < 0$.
  Find the values of x for which $y < 0$. Look for the values of x when the graph is below the x-axis.
  The values are $-0.7 < x < 1.7$.

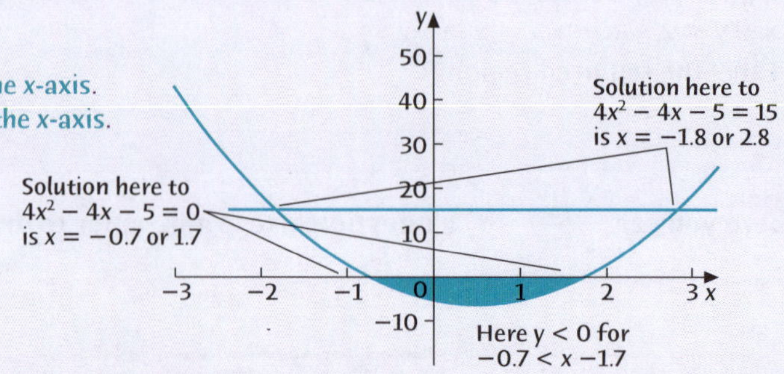

The Crash Course

Solution of simultaneous equations using graphs

Plot each equation as a separate line. Where the two graphs intersect the **x-value** and **y-value** are true for both equations. Find the solution by reading off the **x-** and **y-values** at the point of intersection.

Example

Solve the simultaneous equations $y + 2x = 4$ and $y - x = 2$.
The graph of the first line has already been drawn.
For the second equation add x to both sides to make y the subject, $y = x + 2$.
Make a table of values for $y = x + 2$.

x	−2	0	2
y	0	2	4

Remember for a straight line, you only need to plot three points.

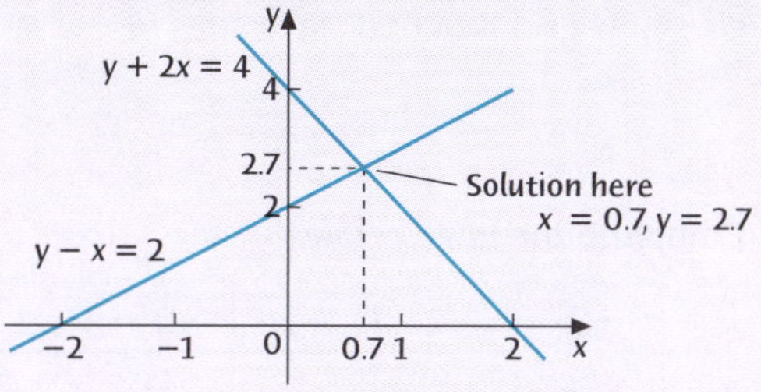

Inequalities on graphs

To show inequalities on a graph first plot the boundary line. If the inequality is $>$ or $<$ use a dotted boundary line to show the line is not included. If the inequality is $\leqslant$ or $\geqslant$ use a solid boundary line to show the line is included. Read the question carefully and check which region must be shaded.

Example

Show $y < 2x + 3$ and $y \geqslant -4$ on a graph.
Plot $y = 2x + 3$ as a broken line and $y = -4$ as a solid line.

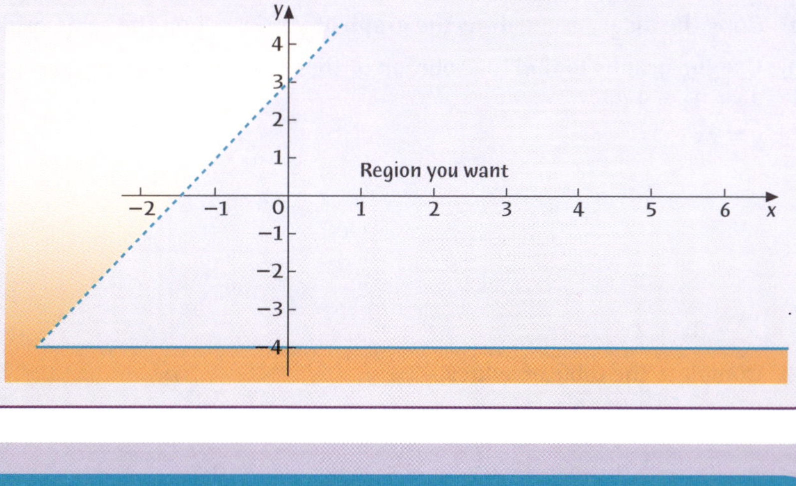

Key facts and skills

When plotting graphs:

- first make a **table of values**
- then **plot corresponding x- and y-values**
- **join the points** in a straight line or a smooth curve

When solving equations:

- **plot the left- and right-hand side** of the equation
- find the **point of intersection** of the two graphs and take the x-value

When solving simultaneous equations:

- **plot both equations**
- find the **point of intersection** and take the x- and y-values

When showing linear inequalities:

- **plot the line of the equation**
- use **dotted lines for < and >**, use **solid lines for ⩽ and ⩾**
- **shade the appropriate region**

Exam Practice Questions

1 a) Use the formula $y = 2x + 1$ to complete the table.

x	-1	0	1	2
$y = 2x + 1$		1		

b) Use the table of values to draw the graph of $y = 2x + 1$ on graph paper.

c) Use your graph to find the values of x when $y = 3.5$.

2 $y = x^2 - 1$

a) Complete the table below.

x	-3	-2	-1	0	1	2	3
y				-1			8

b) Plot these points on graph paper and draw the graph of $y = x^2 - 1$.

c) Use your graph to find the values of x when $y = 5$.

3 a) Draw a set of axes and plot the graph of $y = x^2 - 3x + 1$ for values of x from -2 to $+3$.

b) Use the graph to find the solutions of the equation $x^2 - 3x = -1$.

c) Use the graph to solve the inequality $x^2 - 3x + 1 < 0$.

d) What is the minimum value of y?

4 The graph of the equation $2y + 3x = 9$ has been drawn on the grid.

a) Copy the diagram and draw the graph of $y = 2x - 1$ on the same grid.

b) Use the graphs to find the solution of these simultaneous equations.

$2y + 3x = 9$

$y = 2x - 1$

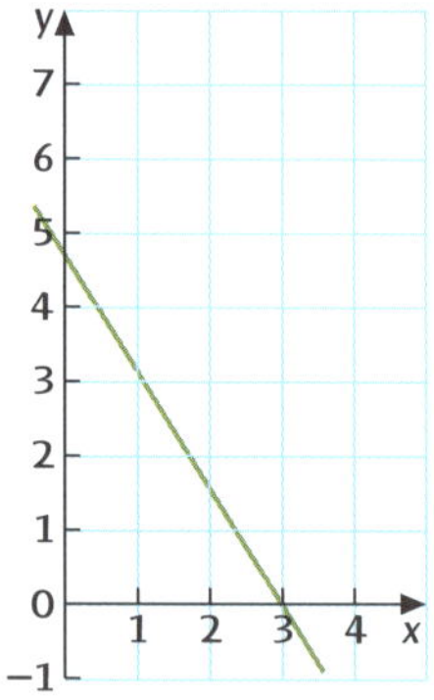

5 $y = x^3 - 3x - 2$

a) Complete the table of values.

x	-2	-1	0	1	2	3
y		0	-2			16

b) Using graph paper draw the graph of $y = x^3 - 3x - 2$.

c) By drawing a suitable straight line on your graph, estimate the solutions to the equation $x^3 - 3x - 2 = -1$.

6 The shaded region satisfies three inequalities. Write them down.

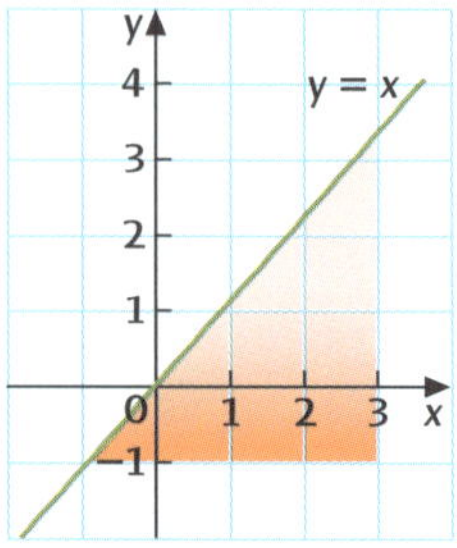

Revision Unit 9

Gradients and lines

The Check Up

1 Find the equation of the line in each of these diagrams.

a)

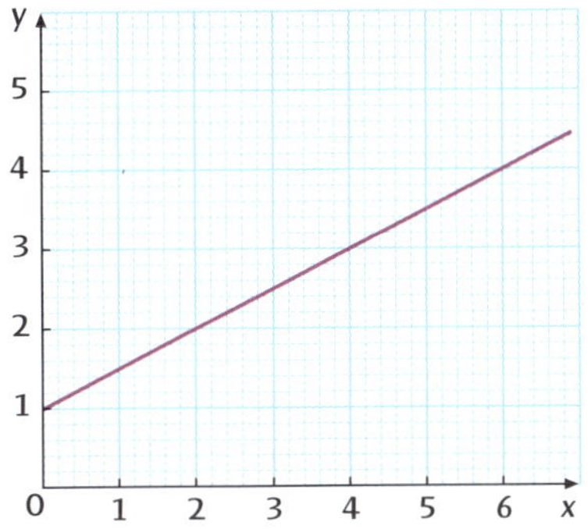

____

b)

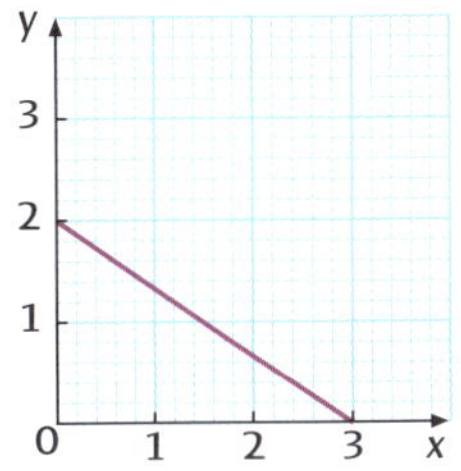

____

2 The line $y = 3x + 1$ is drawn on these axes.
Draw a line parallel to this line, passing through the point (1, 2).

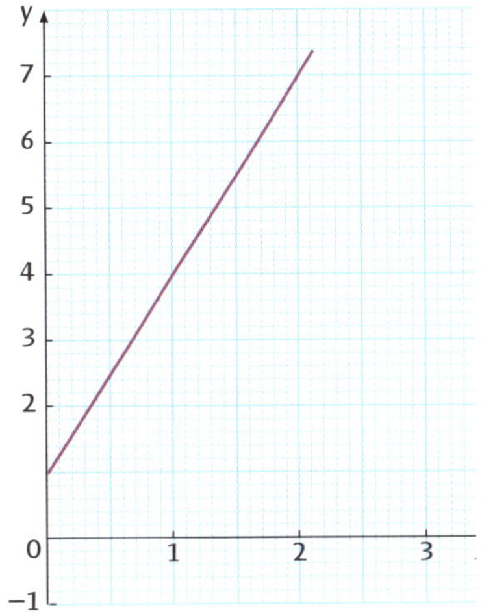

Write down the equation of this line. ______________

3 The diagram shows the travel graph of a car.
How long after the start of its journey did the car first stop and for how long? ______________
What was the greatest speed of the car? ______________

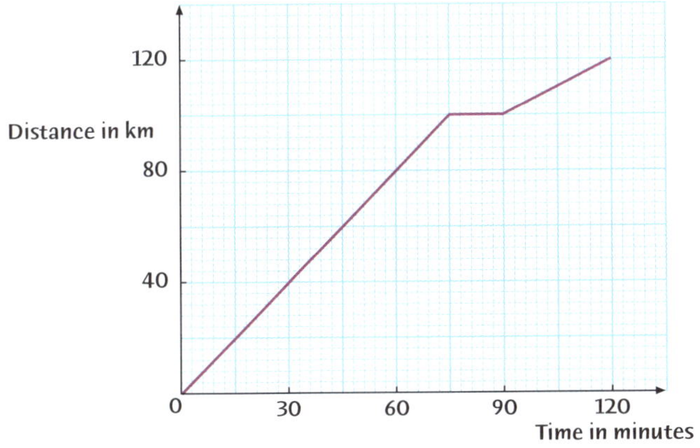

4 The two graphs show the population changes in two small villages of Goss and Den over 10 years. Describe fully what is happening to the population in each village.

____

____

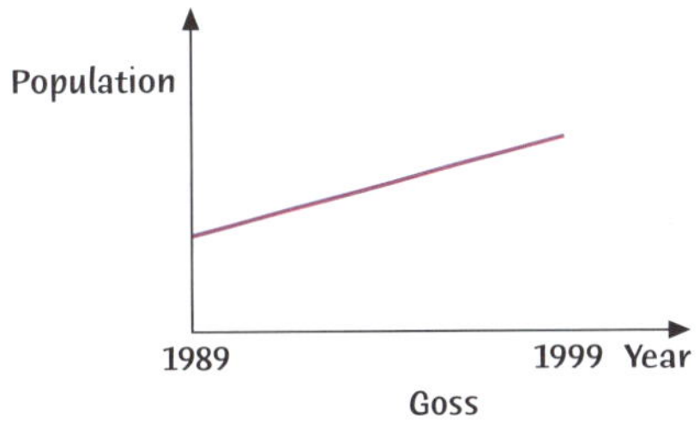

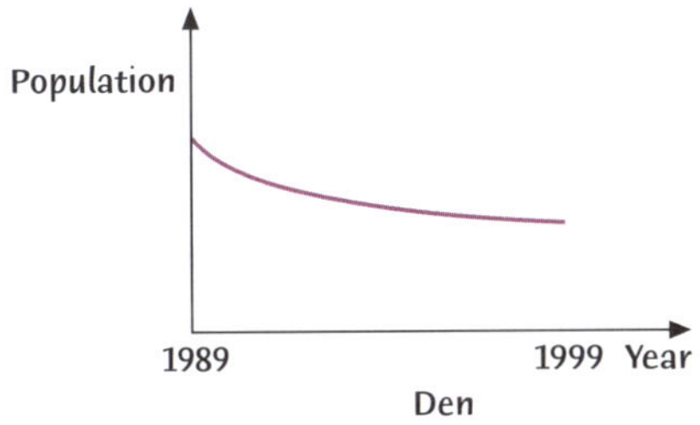

Mark yourself *(see answers on page 102)*

- **Just a few wrong?** You're geared up for the Exam Practice Questions. Go for it!
- **More than a few wrong?** Boost your learning powers by taking the Crash Course before you tackle the Exam Practice Questions.

/ 8

GRADIENTS AND LINES

THE CRASH COURSE

Gradient of a line

The gradient of a line is a measure of its steepness. The letter 'm' is usually used for the gradient of a line.
To work out the gradient of a line draw a step like this.
Now find the gradient of line AB using the formula:

$m = \frac{\text{y-step}}{\text{x-step}}$ or $m = \frac{\text{vertical step}}{\text{horizontal step}}$

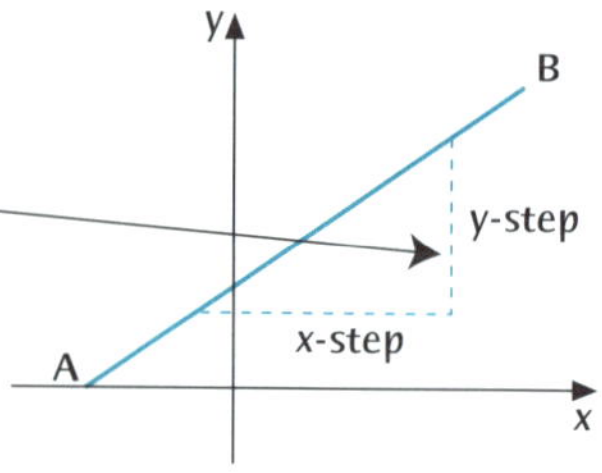

If m is large the line looks like this: / If m is small the line looks like this:

If m is negative the line looks like this: \ or

Tip: If m is the same in two or more lines they are parallel like this: /// or like this: \\\

The straight line $y = mx + c$

Any straight line can be written in the form $y = mx + c$.
In the equation $y = mx + c$, m is the gradient and c is where the line cuts the y-axis (the y-intercept).

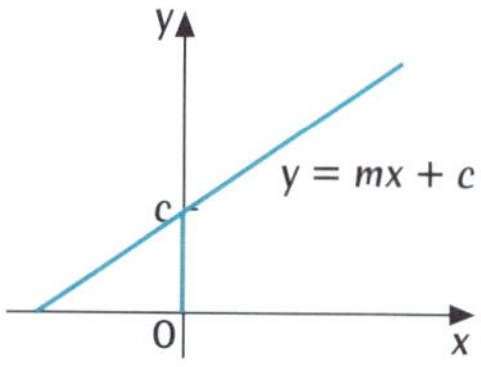

Steps for finding the equation of a given straight line

1 First draw a step on the line to work out the gradient.

Tip: Remember if the line is like this / m is +, and if the line is like this \ m is −.

2 Find the value of y where the line cuts the y-axis. This is c.

3 Use $y = mx + c$ which gives y = gradient × x + value where line cuts the y-axis.
If the line goes through the origin $c = 0$ so y = gradient × x.

EXAMPLE

The line graph shows the cost of gas, P, calculated from the number of therms of gas used T. Find the equation of the line.
What does the gradient represent?
The graph is a straight line so use $y = mx + c$
where $y = P$ and $x = T$.

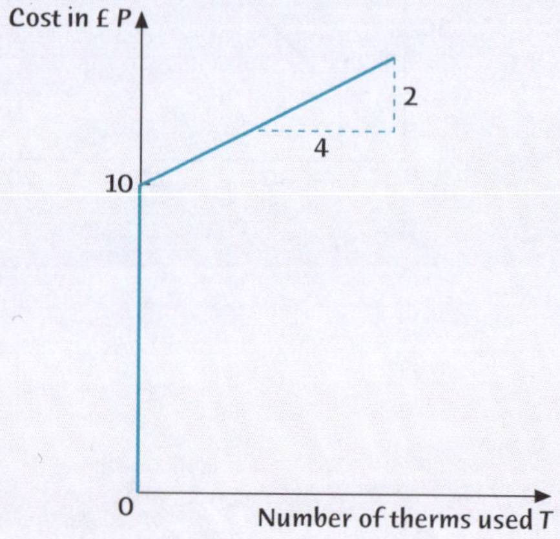

1 To find m, draw a step and work out the vertical and horizontal part of the step.

m is positive, $m = \frac{\text{vertical step}}{\text{horizontal step}}$

$= \frac{2}{4}$

$= 0.5$

2 To find c, look where the line cuts the vertical axis:
$c = 10$

3 Now substitute $y = P$, $x = T$, $m = 0.5$ and $c = 10$ in the equation $y = mx + c$ to find the equation of the line.
$P = 0.5T + 10$

The units of the gradient are $\frac{P\text{ units}}{T\text{ units}} = \frac{\text{pounds (£)}}{\text{number of therms}}$

The gradient is the **cost per therm**.

THE CRASH COURSE

Distance-time graphs

For these graphs plot the distance on the vertical axis and time on the horizontal axis.

The gradient of the graph gives the speed.

$$\text{Gradient} = \frac{\text{distance step}}{\text{time step}} = \text{speed (units m/s)}$$

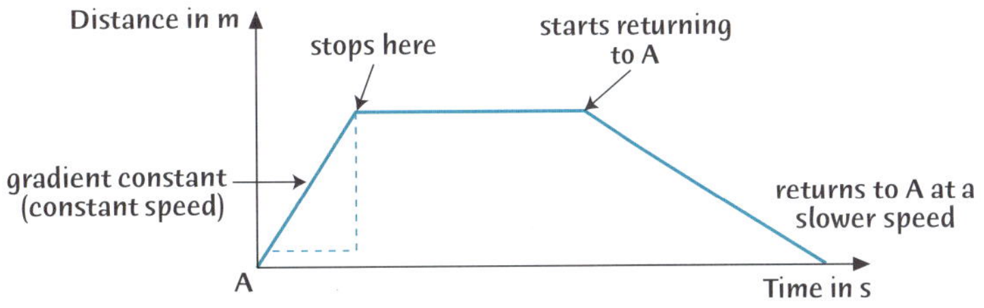

EXAMPLE

Use this graph to describe the race between Joe and Andrew, starting at A and finishing at B.
Andrew runs at a steady speed of 6 m/s throughout the race.
Joe starts off running slowly, then he increases his speed and passes Andrew. Unfortunately he gets a stitch and has to stop for about 30 seconds, during which time Andrew passes him. He then puts on a final spurt passing Andrew to reach the finishing line about 5 seconds before him.

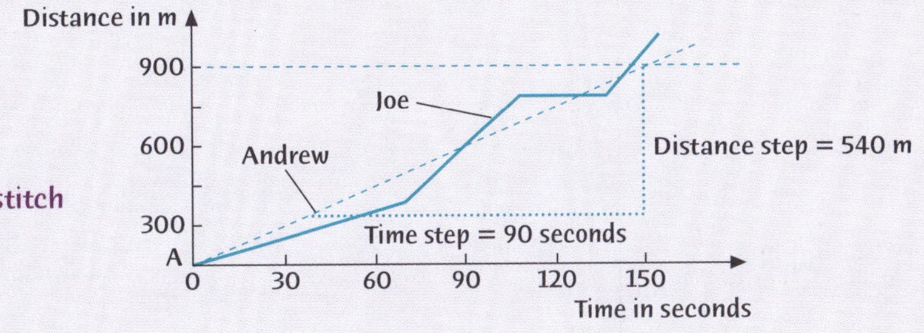

Graphs in other practical situations

The gradients can be useful in interpreting various graphs

EXAMPLE

The containers 1, 2 and 3 are filled with water at a constant rate. The three graphs show the depth of water (d) on the vertical axis and the time (t) on the horizontal axis. Match the graphs to the containers.
Container 1 has parallel sides, so the water rises at a steady or constant rate.
Container 2 has curves sides, becoming further apart. At first the water rises quickly, then slows down.
Container 3 has sides that slope inwards, then become parallel, so the water rises slowly at first, then at a constant rate.

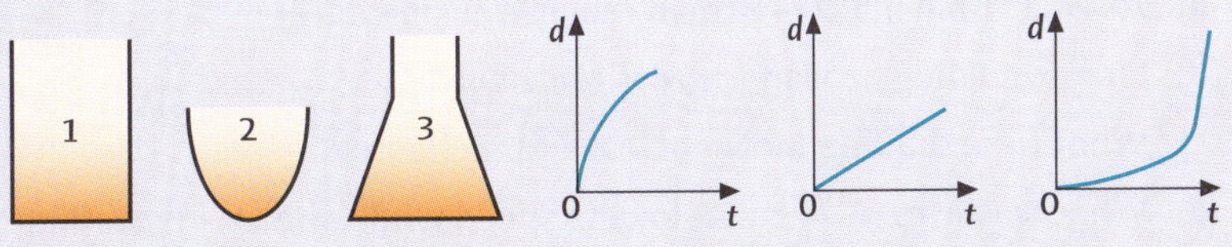

The solution is:

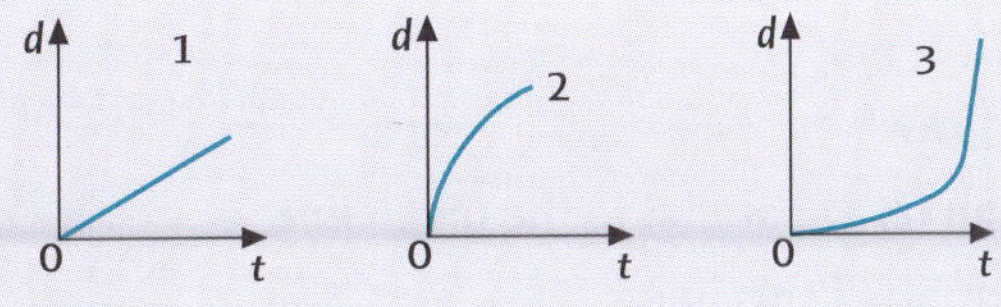

KEY FACTS AND SKILLS

- the gradient of a straight line is 'y-step' ÷ 'x-step'
- the general equation of a straight line is $y = mx + c$ where m is the gradient and c is the y-intercept
- in distance-time graphs the gradient is the speed
- for other graphs in practical situations, think about what the gradient is doing

Exam Practice Questions

1 This graph shows the cost of hiring a car, which is a fixed amount and a charge for the number of miles travelled.

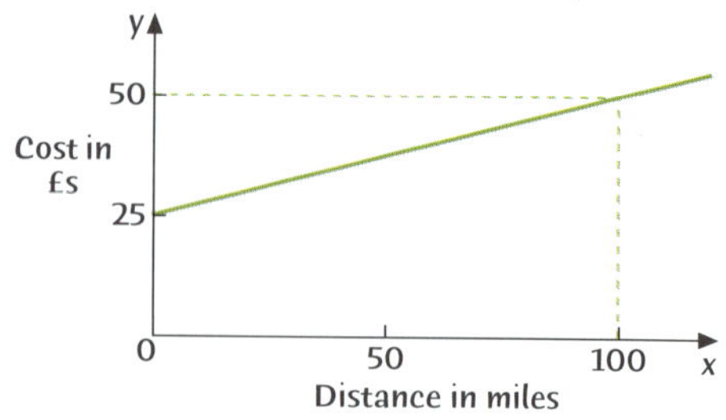

a) What is the fixed charge?

b) Find the equation of the line in the form $y = mx + c$.

c) How much does it cost to travel 150 miles?

2 The solid line shows part of Mrs Brown's journey from Newcastle to Manchester. The dotted line shows Mrs McNicol's journey from Manchester to Newcastle. They arrange to meet at Wayside café.

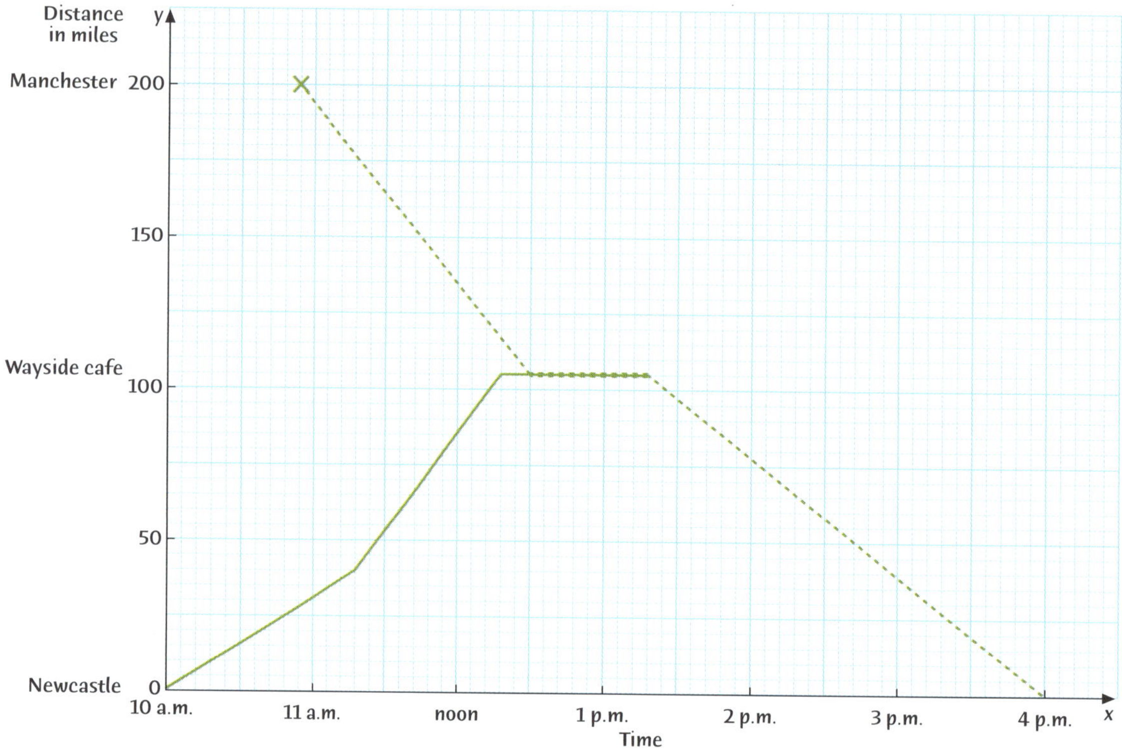

a) At what time did Mrs Brown reach Wayside café?

b) How long did she wait for Mrs McNicol?

c) What time did Mrs McNicol leave Manchester?

d) What was Mrs McNicol's slowest speed while she was travelling?

e) They left the café at the same time and Mrs Brown continued on to Manchester, travelling at a steady 60 mph. Draw this part of the journey.

3 The line $y = -2x + 4$ is drawn on the axes.

a) Draw the line through (2, 4) parallel to the given line.

b) Write down the equation of this line.

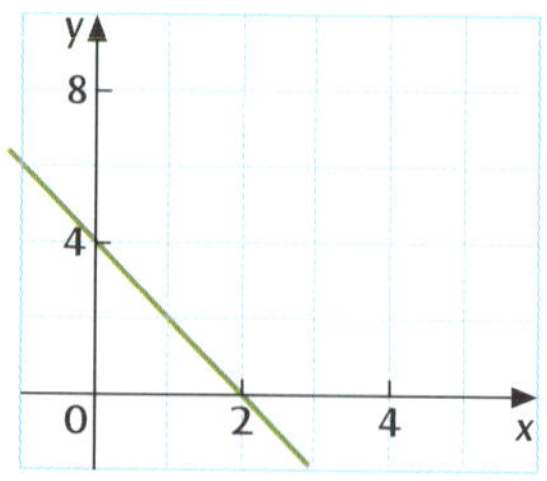

Revision Unit 10

Solving more equations

The Check Up

1 Solve these simultaneous equations.

$3a + 4b = 6$ $a =$ ______

$a + 2b = 4$ $b =$ ______

2 Solve these simultaneous equations.

$2y + 3x = 9$ $x =$ ______

$3y - 5x = 4$ $y =$ ______

3 Ahmed spent £5.80 on five cups of coffee and three cups of tea. Jack spent £6.20 on four cups of coffee and five cups of tea. If c pence is the price of coffee and t pence is the price of tea, make two equations and solve them to find the cost of one cup of coffee and one cup of tea.

______

______

$t =$ ______

$c =$ ______

4 Using a trial and improvement method to solve this equation.

$x^3 - 2x = 15$ ______

Give your answer to 2 d.p.

Mark yourself *(see answers on page 103)*

- Just a few wrong? You're geared up for the Exam Practice Questions. Go for it!
- More than a few wrong? Boost your learning powers by taking the Crash Course before you tackle the Exam Practice Questions.

/ 9

THE CRASH COURSE

Simultaneous equations

$3x + 5y = 16$ and $2x + 4y = 41$ are **simultaneous equations**.
The two equations have two unknowns, in this case x and y. To solve the equations, find the values of x and y which satisfy both equations, or make them both true, at the same time.

Tip: Simultaneous means 'at the same time'.

Making simultaneous equations

Write the information that is given, in two equations, using two different letters for the numbers that are to be found.

EXAMPLE

Jack buys three cans of Tang and two cans of Zest which cost him altogether £1.46.
Elanor buys one can of Tang and four cans of Zest which cost her £1.32.
Write the information as two equations.
Let x be the number of cans of Tang and y be the number of cans of Zest.
The equation for Jack is $3x + 2y = 146$ (working in pence).
The equation for Elanor is $x + 4y = 132$.

Steps for solving simultaneous equations

Solve these simultaneous equations.
$3x + 2y = 146 \quad x + 4y = 132$

1 Make the numbers in front of either the x- or y-terms the same.

Tip: It is useful to know that this number is called the x- or y-coefficient.

Choosing the y-term, multiply the first equation by 2.
First equation $(3x + 2y = 146) \times 2 \rightarrow 6x + 4y = 292$
Second equation $x + 4y = 132$

2 Now get rid of the chosen term.

Tip: If the chosen terms have the same signs subtract the equations.
If the chosen terms have different signs add the equations.

The chosen y-terms have the same signs, so subtract the equations.

$$\begin{array}{r} 6x + 4y = 292 \\ x + 4y = 132 \\ \hline 5x \qquad = 160 \end{array}$$

3 Solve the linear equation to find x.
To get rid of the the 'multiply by 5' divide each side by 5: $x = 32$

4 Put this value of x in the first equation to find y.
$3x + 2y = 146$
$3 \times 32 + 2y = 146$
$96 + 2y = 146$
To get rid of the '+96' subtract 96 from each side: $2y = 146 - 96 = 50$
To get rid of the 'multiply by 2' divide each side by 2: $y = 25$

5 Check that these values work in the second equation.
$x + 4y = 132 \rightarrow 32 + 4 \times 25 = 132$ ✓
Solution $x = 32$, $y = 25$.

THE CRASH COURSE

More difficult simultaneous equations

Sometimes it is necessary to multiply both equations by different numbers to make the coefficients of one term the same. Then the steps are the same as for any other pair of simultaneous equations.

EXAMPLE

Solve the simultaneous equations $2x + 3y = 9$ and $5x + 2y = 17$.

1 Choose to make the y-coefficients the same.
Multiply $2x + 3y = 9$ by 2: $4x + 6y = 18$
Multiply $5x + 2y = 17$ by 3: $15x + 6y = 51$

2 The y-terms have the same signs so subtract the equations to eliminate them.

$$\begin{aligned} 15x + 6y &= 51 \\ 4x + 6y &= 18 \\ \hline 11x \quad\quad &= 33 \end{aligned}$$

3 Solve the linear equation to find x.
Divide both sides by 11: $x = 3$

4 Put this value of x in the first equation to find y.

$$\begin{aligned} 2 \times 3 + 3y &= 9 \\ 6 + 3y &= 9 \\ 3y &= 9 - 6 = 3 \\ y &= 1 \end{aligned}$$

5 Check that these values work in equation 2. $5x + 2y = 17 \rightarrow 5 \times 3 + 2 \times 1 = 17$ ✓
Solution $x = 3$, $y = 1$.

Other equations

Some equations, such as cubic equations, can be solved using a trial and improvement method.

Cubic equations

A cubic equation must have a cubed term. Two examples of cubic equations are $x^3 - x^2 = 10$ and $x^3 + 2x - 1 = 0$. These examples each have a term with x^3.

Solving a cubic equation using a trial and improvement method

This method involves making sensible 'guesses' at the value of the unknown, then trying to improve the guess until a solution is found.

EXAMPLE

Using a trial and improvement method, solve $y^3 - y^2 = 20$ giving the answer to 1 d.p.

First find the two integer values between which the solution lies.

Try $y = 2$: $2^3 - 2^2 = 4$ too small
Try $y = 3$: $3^3 - 3^2 = 18$ too small
Try $y = 4$: $4^3 - 4^2 = 48$ too big

The answer is nearer 3 than 4 so now try $y = 3.2$.

Try $y = 3.2$: $3.2^3 - 3.2^2 = 22.5$ too big
Try $y = 3.1$: $3.1^3 - 3.1^2 = 20.2$ still too big

The answer lies between 3 and 3.1 so try $y = 3.05$.

Try $y = 3.05$: $3.05^3 - 3.05^2 = 19.1$ too small

So the answer lies between 3.1 and 3.05. Correct to 1 d.p. these are the same so the answer is 3.1.

KEY FACTS AND SKILLS

- to solve **linear simultaneous equations**
  first **make the coefficients of one of the letter-terms the same**
  then **eliminate (get rid of) that term** by subtracting or adding
  then **solve a linear equation** to find the remaining letter
  find the second letter by **substitution**
- to solve other equations, use a **trial and improvement method**

EXAM PRACTICE QUESTIONS

1 The sum of two numbers is 33 and the difference between the two numbers is 25.
The larger number is l and the smaller number is s.
Find the smaller number.

2 Solve the following simultaneous equations.
$3a + 2b = 13$
$5a - b = 26$

3 The height h, of a ball at time t is given by the equation $h = at + bt^2$.

a) If $h = 20$ when $t = 1$, and $h = 30$ when $t = 3$ find two simultaneous equations for a and b.

b) Now solve your equations to find a and b.

4 Solve the following simultaneous equations.
$4x + 7y = 7$
$6x - 2y = 23$

5 Use a trial and improvement method to find the solution of the equation $x^3 + 4x = 60$, to 1 d.p.

Revision Unit 11

Sequences

The Check Up

1 Write down the next two terms and the *n*th term in each sequence.

a) 3, 9, 15, 21, … ____ ____ ________

b) 8, 5, 2, −1, … ____ ____ ________

c) 1, 8, 27, 64, … ____ ____ ________

2 Write down the next two terms and the *n*th term in this sequence.

2, 5, 10, 17, 26, … ____ ____ ________

3 Write down the next two terms in this sequence.

2, 3, 5, 8, 13, … ____ ____

4 Use the method of differences to find the next two terms in this sequence.

11, 15, 22, 32, 45, … ____ ____

Mark yourself *(see answers on page 103)*

- Just a few wrong? You're geared up for the Exam Practice Questions. Go for it!
- More than a few wrong? Boost your learning powers by taking the Crash Course before you tackle the Exam Practice Questions.

/16

The Crash Course

Definition

A sequence is an **ordered** set of numbers that obey a rule. The task is usually to work out the rule, then find two more terms and the nth term. It is often easy to work out the rule and describe it in words. It may be more difficult to find the general or nth term.

Common sequences

- 1, 4, 9, ... are the **square numbers**; they can also be written as $1^2, 2^2, 3^2, \ldots$
  The fourth term is $4^2 = 16$, the fifth term is $5^2 = 25$, the twentieth term is $20^2 = 400$.
  The nth term is n^2.
  The sequence 0, 3, 8, 15,... is 'one less than the square numbers'. The nth term is $n^2 - 1$.
- 1, 8, 27, ... are the **cube numbers**, they can also be written as $1^3, 2^3, 3^3, \ldots$
  The fourth term is $4^3 = 64$, the fifth term is $5^3 = 125$, the twentieth term is $20^3 = 8000$. The nth term is n^3.
- $\frac{1}{2}, \frac{2}{3}, \frac{3}{4}, \ldots$
  The fourth term is $\frac{4}{5}$, the fifth term is $\frac{5}{6}$, the twentieth term is $\frac{20}{21}$. The nth term is $\dfrac{n}{n+1}$.

Tip: Look for sequences based on the square numbers.

Fibonacci sequences

Each term is found by adding the previous two terms.

- 1, 1, 2, 3, 5, ... the sixth term is $3 + 5 = 8$, the seventh term is $5 + 8 = 13$
- 4, 7, 11, 18, 29, ... the sixth term is $18 + 29 = 47$, the seventh term is $29 + 47 = 76$

Sequences formed by adding the same number (a constant difference)

In a sequence formed by adding on the same number each time:
nth term = first term + $d(n - 1)$ where d is the number added on each time.

Examples

- Find the next two terms and the nth term in the sequence 7, 10, 13, ...
  The rule is 'add on 3' each time, so $d = 3$ and the next two terms are 16 and 19.
  To find the nth term, the first term is 7 and $d = 3$.
  nth term $= 7 + 3(n - 1) = 7 + 3n - 3 = 3n + 4$
- Find the nth term in the sequence 6, 2, −2, ...
  The rule is 'subtract 4' each time, so $d = -4$. The first term is 6.
  nth term $= 6 - 4(n - 1) = 6 - 4n + 4 = -4n + 10$

Tip: d is often called the difference or the constant difference.

Sequences using the method of differences

If the rule is not easy to spot, try the method of differences.
Take the first term from the second, the second from the third, the third from the fourth and so on to see if a pattern emerges. You may have to do this several times.

Example

Find the next term in the sequence 11, 16, 23, 32, 43, ...

	11		16		23		32		43	...	6th term
First differences		5		7		9		11			
Second differences			2		2		2				

So the 6th term is $2 + 11 + 43 = 56$

Key facts and skills

- **square numbers** are $1^2, 2^2, 3^2, \ldots$
- **cube numbers** are $1^3, 2^3, 3^3, \ldots$
- **Fibonacci sequences** are formed by adding the two preceding terms
- in 'add on' sequences:
  the **nth term = first term + $d(n - 1)$**
  where d is the number added on (the difference)
- use the **method of differences** for more complicated sequences

EXAM PRACTICE QUESTIONS

1 These pattern are made of matchsticks.

1st pattern 2nd pattern 3rd pattern

a) Draw the fourth pattern.

b) Complete this table.

Pattern number *n*	1	2	3	4	5	6
Number of matchsticks *s*	3	5	7			

c) Write a formula for the number of matchsticks s in the nth pattern.

d) How many matchsticks are there in the 100th pattern?

2 These designs are made of circles.

1st design 2nd design 3rd design

a) Draw the fourth design.

b) Complete this table.

Design number	1	2	3	4	5	6
Number of circles	1	4	9			

c) How many circles are there in the 20th design?

d) How many circles are there in the *n*th design?

e) Find the next two terms and the *n*th term in this sequence.

3, 6, 11, 18, …

3 Find the next two terms and the *n*th term in each of these sequences.

a) 2, 5, 8, 11, …

b) $\frac{1}{2}, \frac{2}{5}, \frac{3}{8}, \frac{4}{11}, \ldots$

4 Find the next two terms in the sequence 1, 4, 5, 9, 14, …

Revision Unit 12

Angles and lines

The Check Up

1 Find the values of the angles in these figures.

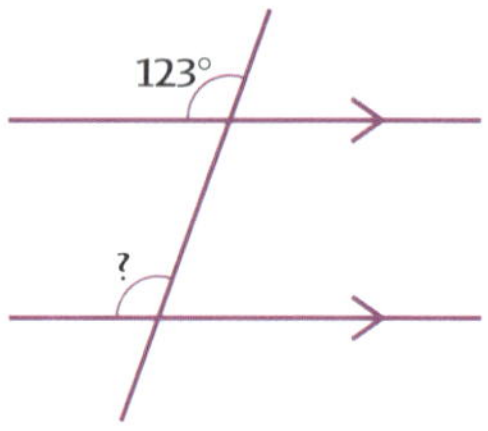

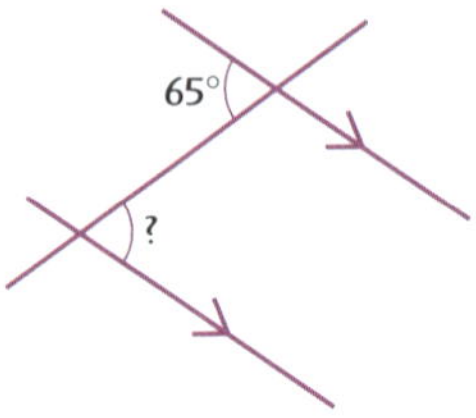

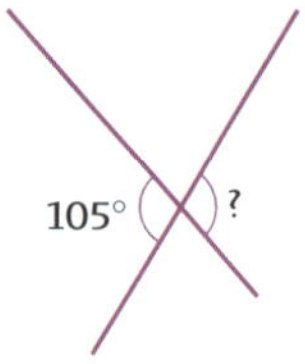

__________ __________ __________

2 Find the size of angle p.

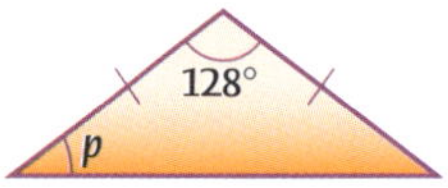

____

3 Find the size of angle q.

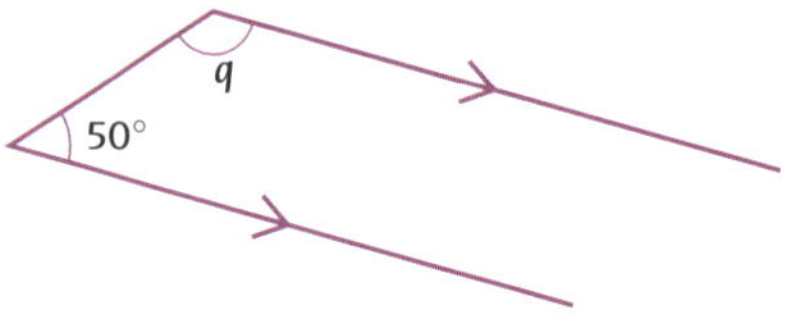

____

4 Find the size of angle r in this quadrilateral.

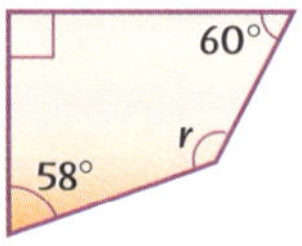

____

5 Find the size of angle s.

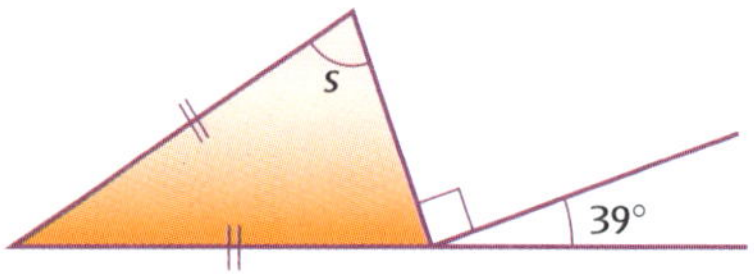

____

6 This is a regular octagon. Find the sizes of angles t and u.

$t =$ __________ $u =$ __________

Is it possible to make a tessellation with this octagon?

____

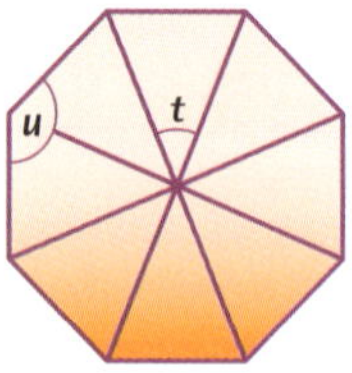

7 Find the bearing of the rock from the boat.

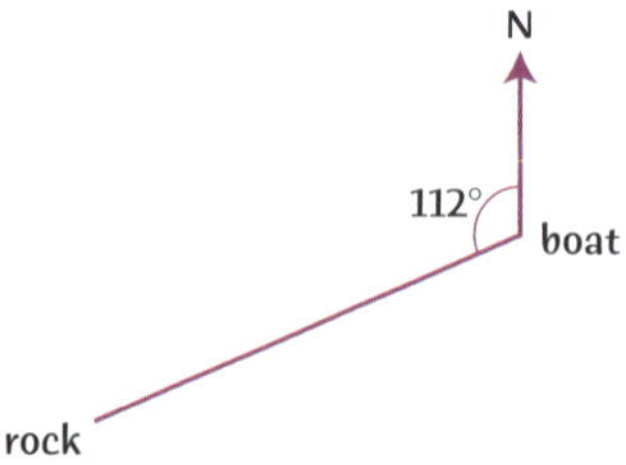

____

Mark yourself *(see answers on page 103)*

- Just a few wrong? You're geared up for the Exam Practice Questions. Go for it!
- More than a few wrong? Boost your learning powers by taking the Crash Course before you tackle the Exam Practice Questions.

/ 11

THE CRASH COURSE

Angles

One **turn** or **revolution** is 360°.

A quarter of a turn is 90° or **one right angle**.

Lines which meet at right angles are **perpendicular**.

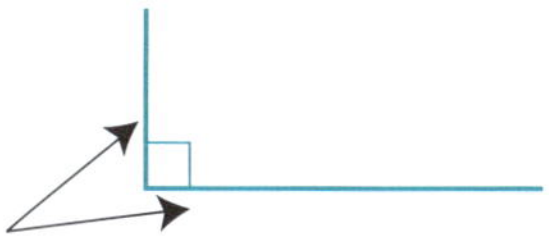

Lines which are a fixed distance apart and never meet are **parallel**.

An **acute angle** is less than 90°.

An **obtuse angle** is greater than 90° but less than 180°.

A **reflex angle** is greater than 180°.

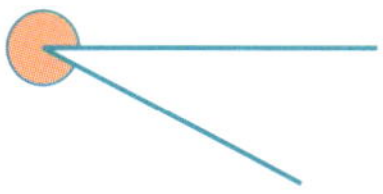

both reflex

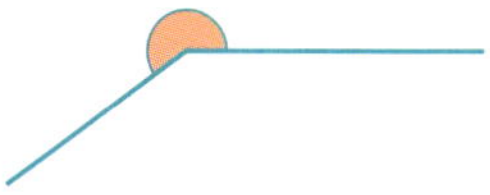

Equal angles

Vertically opposite angles are equal.

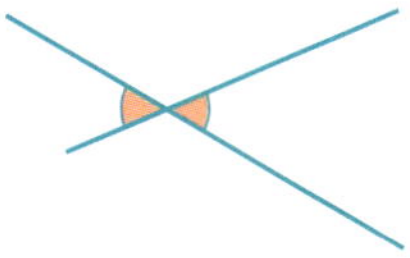

so

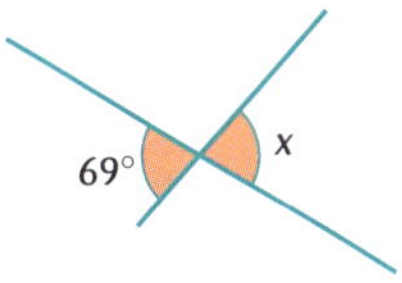

$x = 69°$

Angles and parallel lines

Corresponding angles are equal.
They are sometimes called F angles.

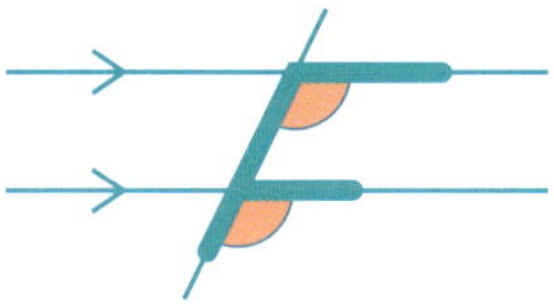

so

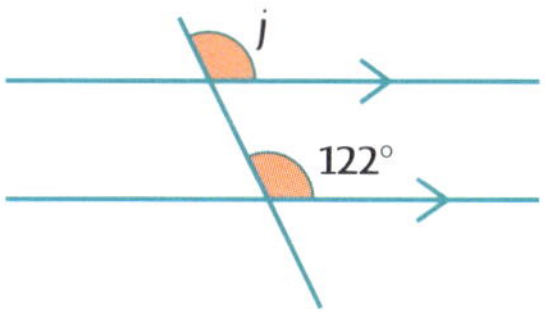

$j = 122°$

Alternate angles are equal.
They are sometimes called Z angles.

so

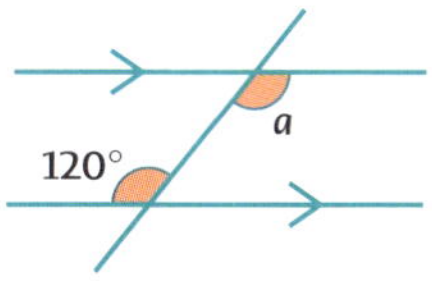

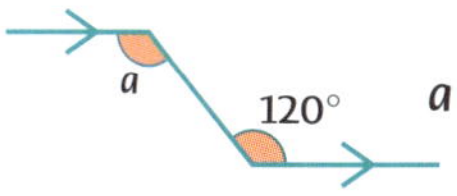

$a = 120°$

Triangles

An **isosceles triangle** has two equal sides and equal angles opposite the equal sides.

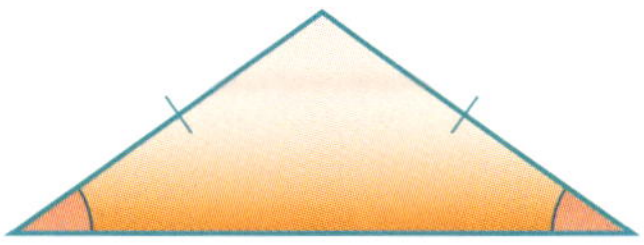

An **equilateral triangle** has all its sides equal and all its angles are equal to 60°.

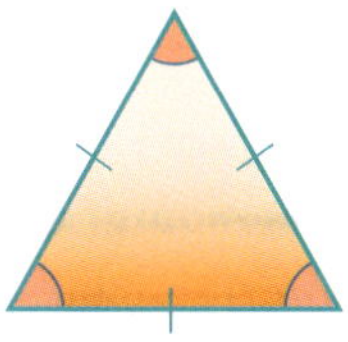

KEY FACTS AND SKILLS

- angles may be **acute**, **right**, **obtuse** or **reflex**
- **vertically opposite angles** are equal
- **corresponding (F) angles** are equal and **alternate (Z) angles** are equal
- an **isosceles triangle** has two equal angles and two equal sides
- an **equilateral triangle** has all sides equal and all angles equal to 60°

THE CRASH COURSE

Angles that add up to 180°

Angles on a straight line add up to 180°.

$x = 180° - 10° - 31° = 139°$

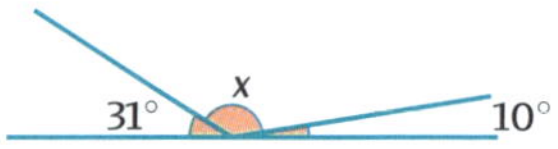

Allied (U) angles add up to 180°.
They may be called co-interior angles.

$y = 180° - 135° = 45°$

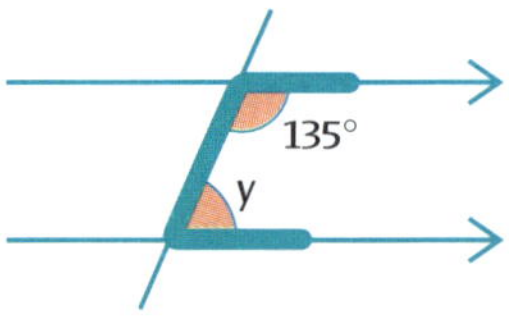

Interior angles of a triangle add up to 180°.

$x + y + z = 180°$

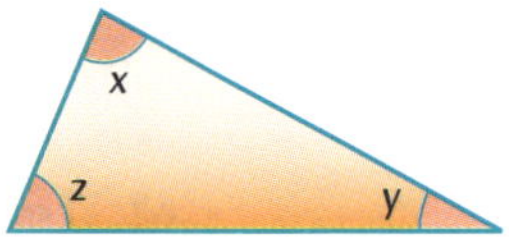

Angles that add up to 360°

Angles at a point add up to 360°.

$a = 360° - 37° - 135° - 80° = 108°$
This result can be used to tell if shapes **tessellate**. Shapes that tessellate must fit together with no gaps. The angles at the point where the shapes meet must add up to 360°.

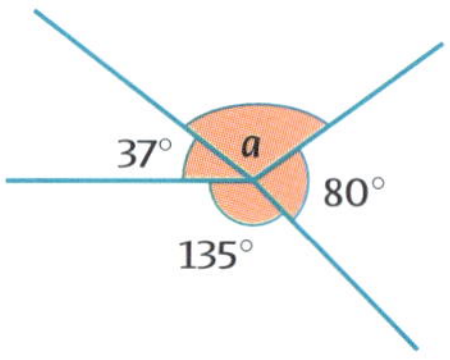

A **quadrilateral** is a figure with four sides.
In any quadrilateral the interior angles add up to 360°.

$z = 360° - 35° - 62° - 108° = 155°$

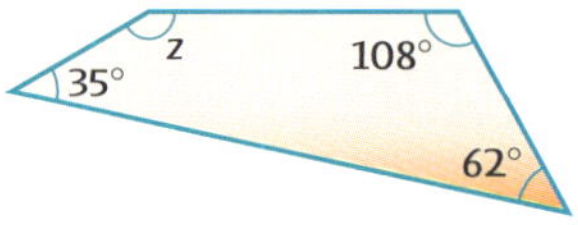

Polygons

A **polygon** is a closed shape with straight sides.
Polygons can be divided into triangles using diagonals.
If the diagonals do not intersect, you can find the sum of the interior angles of the polygon because each triangle has an angle sum of 180°.
This polygon has five sides. It can be divided into three triangles, so the sum of its interior angles is $3 \times 180° = 540°$.

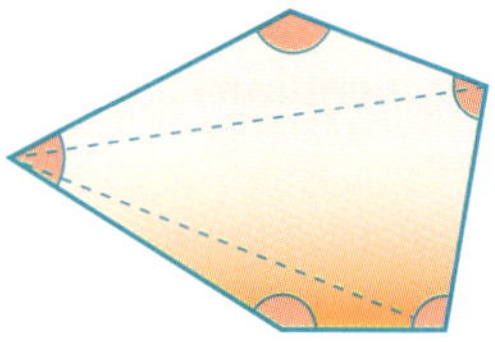

In any polygon the sum of the exterior angles is 360°.
These exterior angles are formed by extending the sides, in order, clockwise or anticlockwise.

$b = 360° - 50° - 101° - 24° - 93° = 92°$
In a **regular polygon**, all the sides are equal, all the interior angles are equal and all the exterior angles are equal.

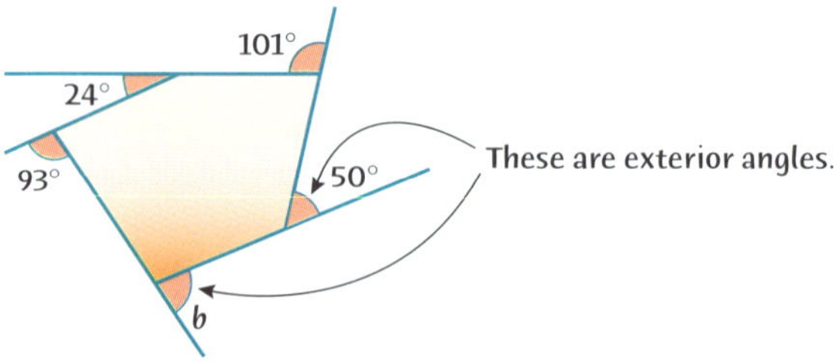

EXAMPLE

In a regular polygon the exterior angles are equal to 30°.
How many sides does the polygon have?
The total of all the exterior angles is 360°.
If the number of sides is n, then $n \times$ (exterior angle) = 360°, so $n \times 30° = 360°$.
The number of sides is $360 \div 30 = 12$

THE CRASH COURSE

Some useful angles

Angle of elevation

This is the angle of elevation from A to the top of the tree.

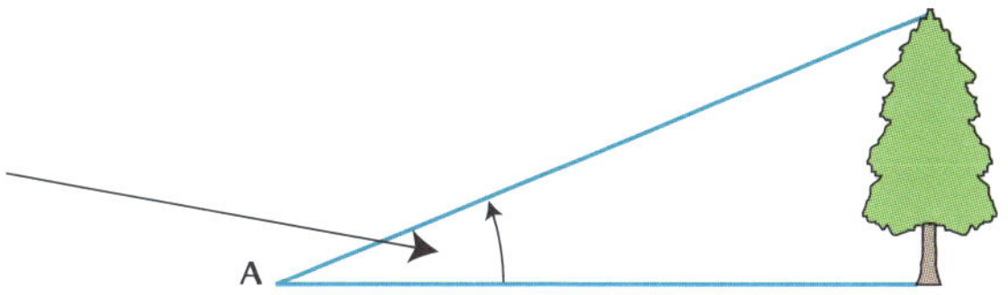

Angle of depression

This is the angle of depression from B to the base of the lighthouse.

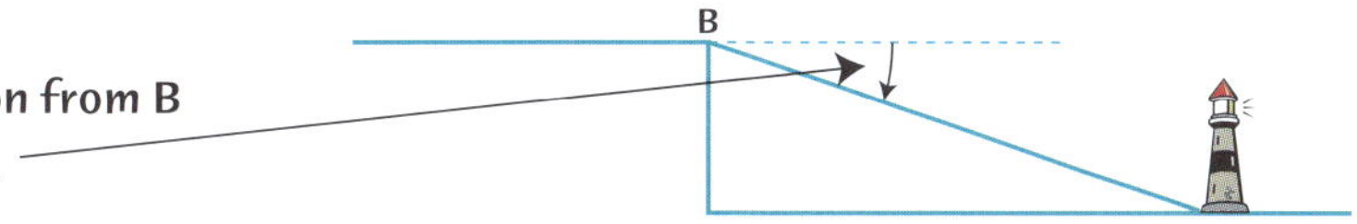

Tip: Angles of elevation and depression are always measured from the **horizontal**.

Bearings

Measuring bearings

The direction of an object from a fixed point can be described by using a three-figure bearing. If the bearing (angle) is less than 100°, put a zero in front of it.

Steps for finding three-figure bearings

Find the bearing of Y from the fixed point X.

1. Draw a north line from the fixed point X.
2. Measure the angle (bearing) from this north line, in a clockwise direction, to Y.
3. Write the bearing, using three figures.
   The bearing of Y from X is 063°.

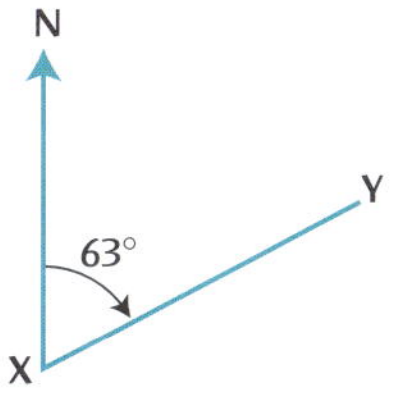

EXAMPLE

The bearing of a boat (B) from a lighthouse (L) is 073°.
Find the bearing of the lighthouse from the boat.

1. Draw the north line at B.
2. This angle is 180° − 73° = 107° (allied angles)
3. The bearing of L from B is 360° − 107° = 253°.

KEY FACTS AND SKILLS

- **angles on a straight line** add up to 180°
- **allied or U angles** add up to 180°
- **interior angles** of a triangle add up to 180° (use this to find the sum of the interior angles of a polygon)
- **angles at a point** add up to 360° (use this to check if shapes tessellate)
- **the sum of the interior angles of a quadrilateral** is 360°
- **the sum of the exterior angles of a polygon** is 360°
- **three-figure bearings** measure the angle starting from the point where the bearing is taken

EXAM PRACTICE QUESTIONS

1 Explain why:

a) angle p is 124°

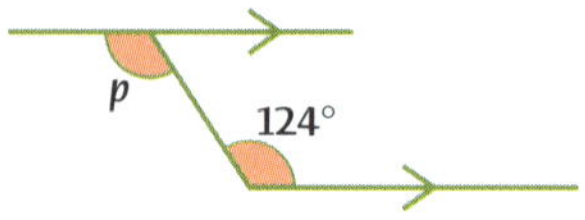

b) angle q is 223°.

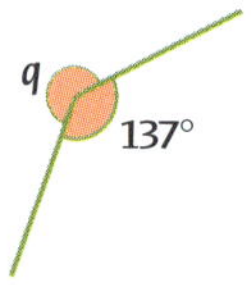

2 Find the values of r, s and t in this figure.

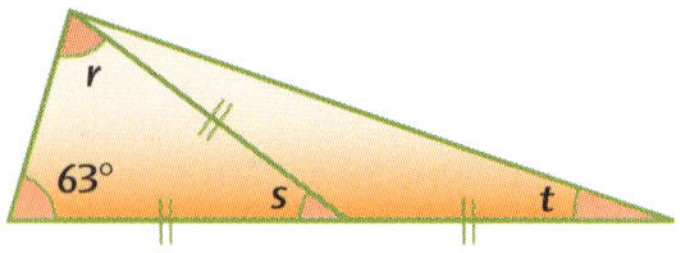

3 a) Find the values of u and v in this regular hexagon.

b) What type of triangle is ABC?

c) Will the shape tessellate? Explain your answer.

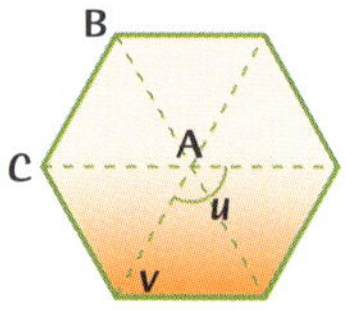

4 a) What is the sum of the interior angles of this seven-sided figure?

b) Angles w, x and z are equal. Find the size of these angles.

c) What kind of angles are w, x and z?

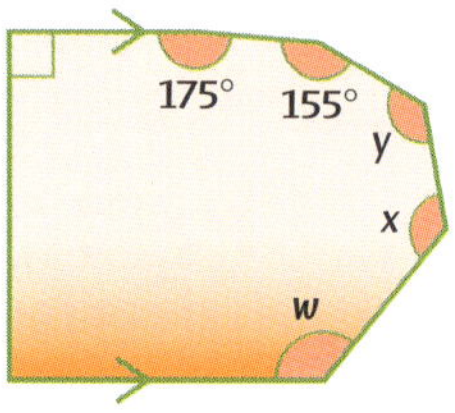

5 X is due north of Y.
From Y the bearing of Z is 051°.
From X the bearing of Z is 112°.
Mark the position of Z.

Revision Unit 13

Transformations

The Check Up

1 Describe fully the transformation that maps A to:

a) B b) C c) D d) E.

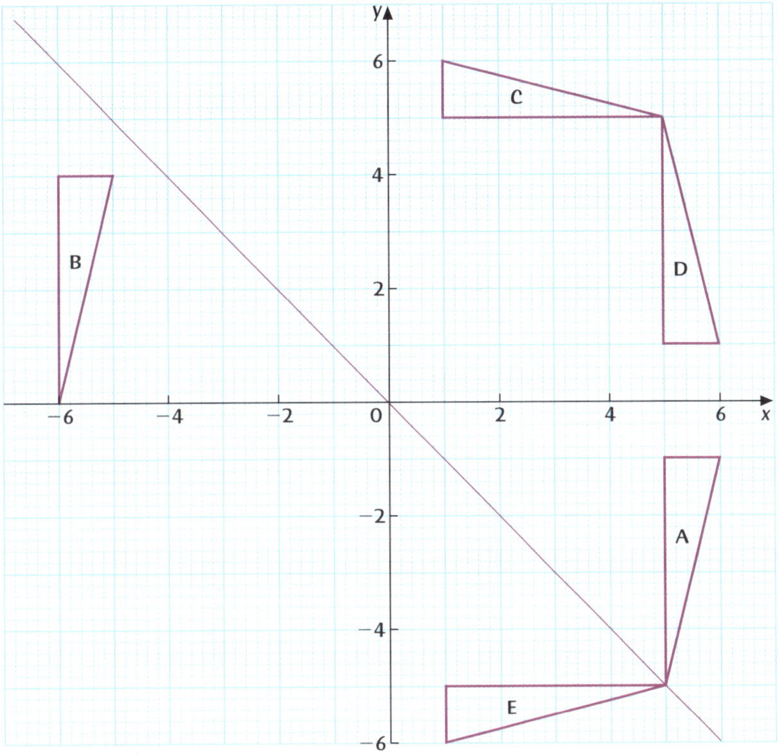

a) ____________

b) ____________

c) ____________

d) ____________

2 a) Enlarge R about centre (1, 1) by scale factor 3.

b) Enlarge R about centre (0, 0) by scale factor $\frac{1}{2}$.

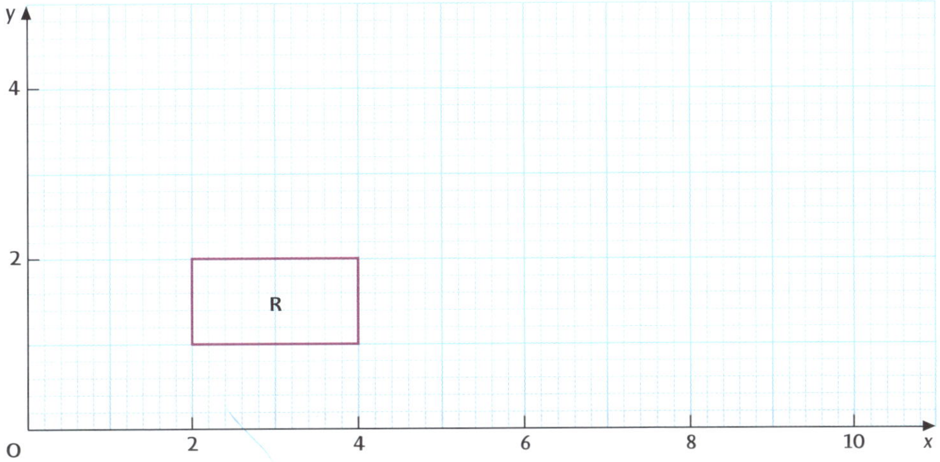

Mark yourself *(see answers on page 103)*

- Just a few wrong? You're geared up for the Exam Practice Questions. Go for it!
- More than a few wrong? Boost your learning powers by taking the Crash Course before you tackle the Exam Practice Questions.

/ 6

THE CRASH COURSE

Definitions

Congruent shapes are exactly the **same shape** and the **same size**. The transformations that produce congruent shapes are **reflections**, **rotations** and **translations**.
Similar shapes are exactly the **same shape** but **different sizes**. The only transformation that produces similar shapes is an **enlargement**.

Reflection

A shape can be reflected in a line called the **line of reflection**. The shape and its reflection are symmetrical about the line.
Shapes are most commonly reflected in the x-axis or the y-axis, or the lines $y = x$ and $y = -x$.

Steps for reflecting an object

To reflect object O in the line $y = x$:

1. Draw a perpendicular from corner A on the object O to the line.
2. Extend this line. Mark a point A' on it, that is the same distance from the line as A.
3. Repeat for the other corners of shape O.
4. Join up the new points, in order, to form the image, I, of the object, O.
5. Check if your drawing is correct by using tracing paper, or by folding along the line of reflection and making sure that the image and object match up.

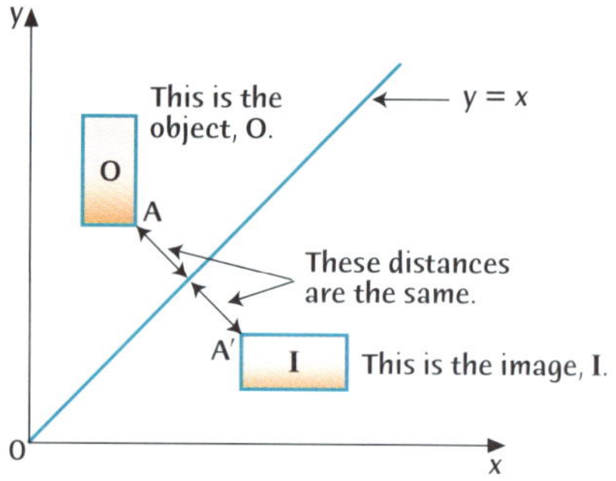

Line of symmetry

Given a symmetrical shape or diagram, it is possible to draw the line of symmetry. This is the line which divides the whole figure into two congruent halves so that one half is the reflection of the other.
The line of symmetry is also called the line of reflection or the mirror line.

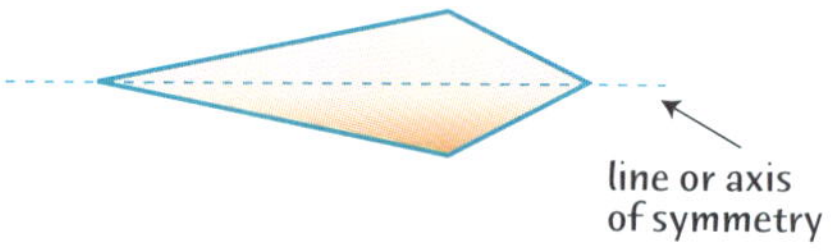

Plane of symmetry

The plane of symmetry divides a 3D shape into two congruent shapes so that one shape is the reflection of the other.

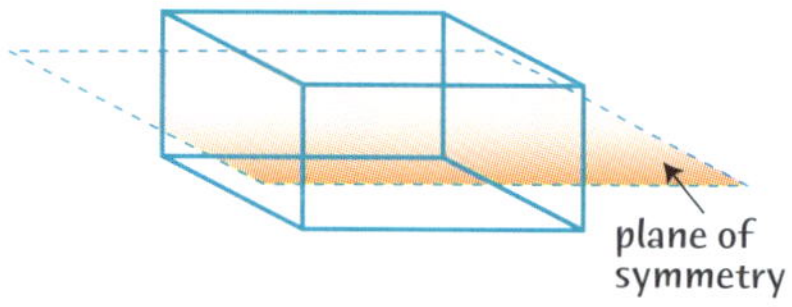

Translation

A translation moves a shape for a given **distance** in a given **direction**.
Column vectors are often used to describe translations. The top number is the distance along and the bottom number is the distance up.

$\begin{pmatrix} 6 \\ 8 \end{pmatrix}$ means 6 units → and 8 units ↑ $\begin{pmatrix} 1 \\ -5 \end{pmatrix}$ means 1 unit → and 5 units ↓

$\begin{pmatrix} -3 \\ 7 \end{pmatrix}$ means 3 units ← and 7 units ↑ $\begin{pmatrix} -2 \\ -9 \end{pmatrix}$ means 2 units ← and 9 units ↓

EXAMPLE

Translate object O by the vector $\begin{pmatrix} 2 \\ 3 \end{pmatrix}$.

- This vector moves object O
  → along 2 units and
  ↑ up three units.

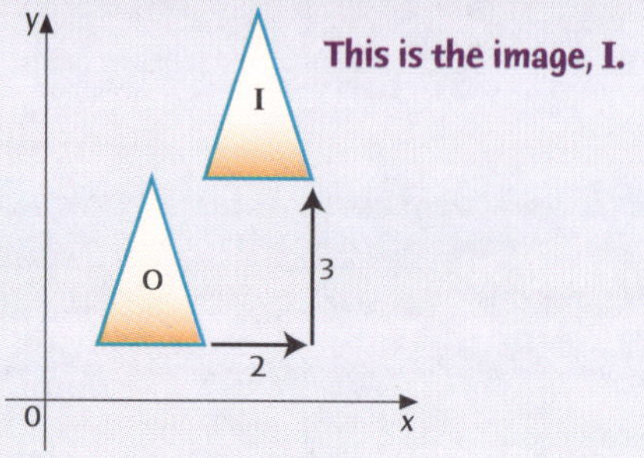

THE CRASH COURSE

Rotation

A shape can be rotated through a **given angle** in a given **direction** about a **given point**.

Steps for rotating an object

Rotate object O about the origin through 90° in a clockwise direction.

1. Measure the distance of point A from the origin along the y-axis, mark point A' the same distance along the x-axis.
2. Now carefully draw the image I congruent to object O.
3. Use tracing paper to check your answer.
   Place the tracing paper over the diagram and trace object O.
   Put the point of a sharp pencil or a pair of compasses at the origin. Carefully turn the tracing paper to move the tracing through 90° clockwise.
   This gives the position of the image.

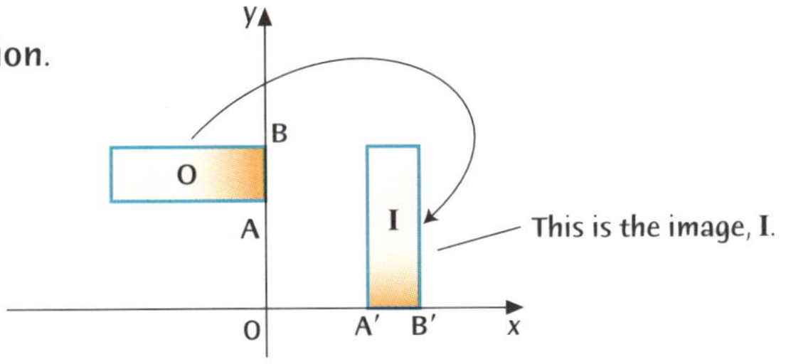

Rotational symmetry

If a shape looks exactly the same when it is rotated about a point, it has rotational symmetry **about that point**. The number of times the shape can be turned, and still look the same, is its **order of rotational symmetry**.

This shape can be turned through 90°, 180°, 270° and 360° and still look the same.

It has rotational symmetry of order 4.

If the shape has to be rotated through 360° before it looks the same it has rotational symmetry of order 1.

Enlargement

A shape can be enlarged by a given **scale factor** about a given **centre of enlargement**. The scale factor is often called k.

Steps for drawing an enlargement

Enlarge the square S about the origin by a scale factor $k = 2$.

1. Draw a line from the origin, the centre of enlargement, to A, a point on the object, and extend it.
2. Measure the distance OA. Multiply this distance by the scale factor, 2, to find the new distance OA'.
3. Repeat for other points on the object.
4. Join up the new points to form the image.

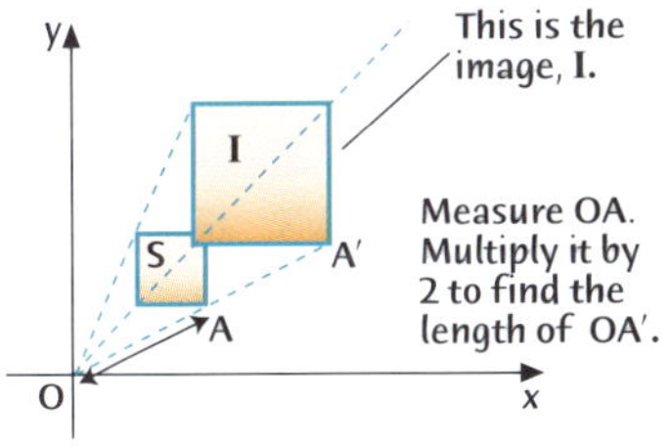

How to describe a given enlargement

To find the centre of enlargement, join two pairs of corresponding points on the object and the image. The point where these two lines intersect is the centre of enlargement.

$$\text{The scale factor is } \frac{\text{length in image}}{\text{corresponding length in object}} = a \div b$$

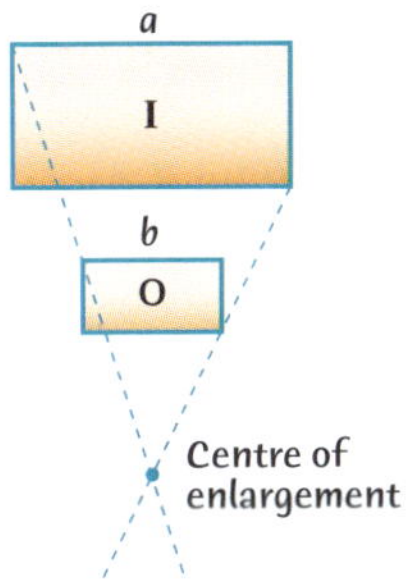

Tip:
If k is a fraction then your enlargement will make the figure smaller.

KEY FACTS AND SKILLS

- **congruent shapes** are identical in shape and size
- a shape may be **reflected**, **rotated** or **translated** to give a congruent shape
- **similar shapes** are identical in shape but not in size
- a shape may be **enlarged** by a **scale factor k** about a **given point**, to give a **similar shape**

EXAM PRACTICE QUESTIONS

1 In the diagram, triangle B is the image of triangle A after an enlargement.

a) Find and label the centre of enlargement, X.

b) Calculate and write down the scale factor of the enlargement.

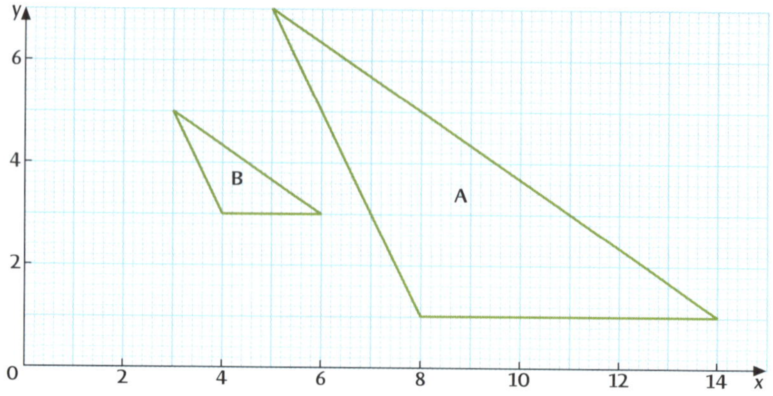

2 Describe a single transformation which moves this object:

a) from position 1 to position 2

b) from position 2 to position 3

c) from position 3 to position 4.

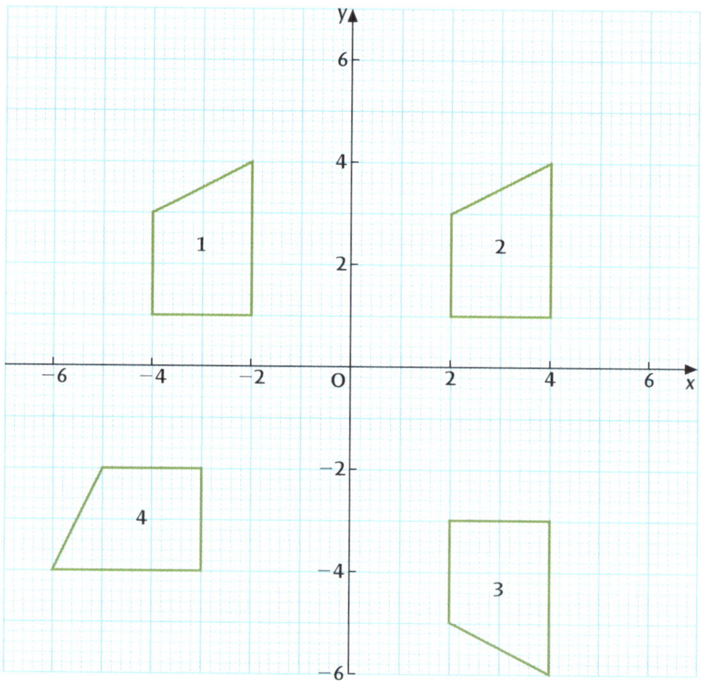

3 Reflect shape A in the line $y = x$.
Label the image B.
Reflect B in the line $y = -x$.
Label the image C.

Translate C by the vector $\begin{pmatrix} 7 \\ -1 \end{pmatrix}$.
Label the image D.

Enlarge D by scale factor 2, centred on $(-1, -1)$. Label the image E

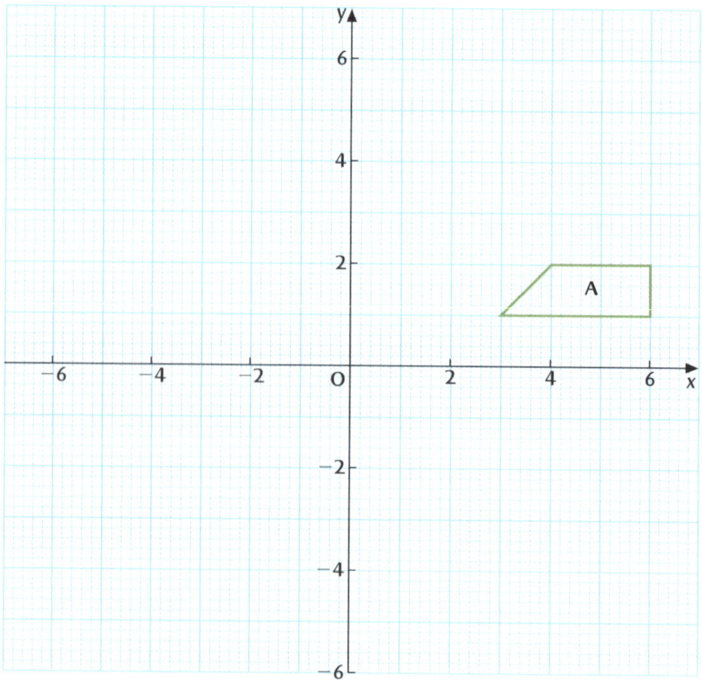

Revision Unit 14

Loci

The Check Up

1 Using only a ruler and compasses, construct the path of a point that stays the same distance between two points A and B.

2 Using only a ruler and compasses, construct an angle of 90°.

3 Using only a ruler and compasses, draw the bisector of this angle.

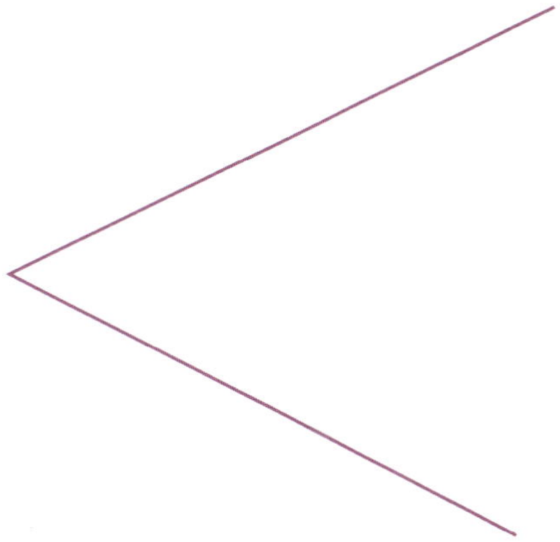

Mark yourself *(see answers on page 104)*

- Just a few wrong? You're geared up for the Exam Practice Questions. Go for it!
- More than a few wrong? Boost your learning powers by taking the Crash Course before you tackle the Exam Practice Questions.

/6

The Crash Course

Definitions

The locus of a point is the path the point makes when it moves following certain conditions. In these diagrams, loci are shown by dotted lines. Loci is the plural of locus.

Movement about one fixed point

The locus of a point which moves so that it is always the same distance, for example 1 cm, from one given fixed point O in a plane, is a circle, radius 1 cm, centre O.
If a conker, on the end of a string of length 8 cm, is whirled around in every direction from a fixed point, it will trace out a path which lies on the surface of a sphere, centred on the fixed point, with radius 8 cm.

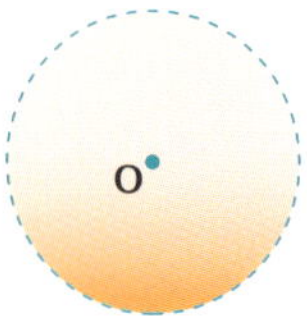

Movement about two fixed points

The locus of a point which moves so that it is always the same distance from two given fixed points, say A and B, is the **perpendicular bisector** of the line joining A to B.

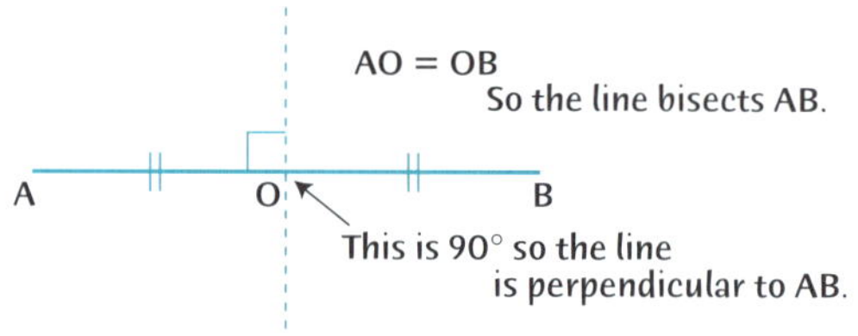

Steps for constructing the perpendicular bisector of a line AB

1 Open the compasses so that the radius is larger than half the length of AB.
2 With the compass point at A draw an arc.
3 With the compass point at B, using the same radius, draw another arc to cut the first one in two places.
4 Join the points where the arcs intersect. This is the perpendicular bisector of AB.

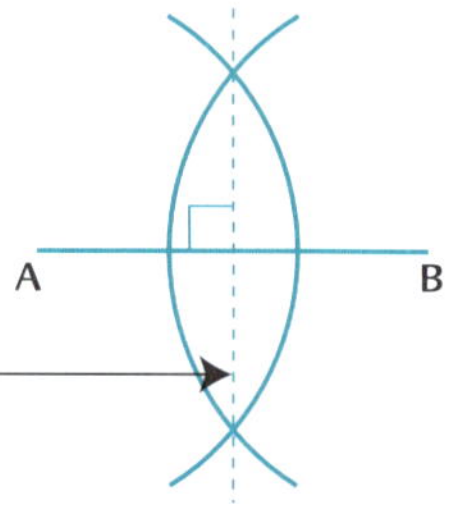

Tip: To construct a right angle, using ruler and compasses only, construct the perpendicular bisector of a line.

How to use loci to find positions

The people in the two villages of Pont and Eland want to build a community centre that is exactly the same distance from the schools in the villages. It most be no more than 3 km from the manager's home. Mark on the plan where the community centre might be.

- Draw the perpendicular bisector of PE.
- The thick line gives the possible positions of the club.

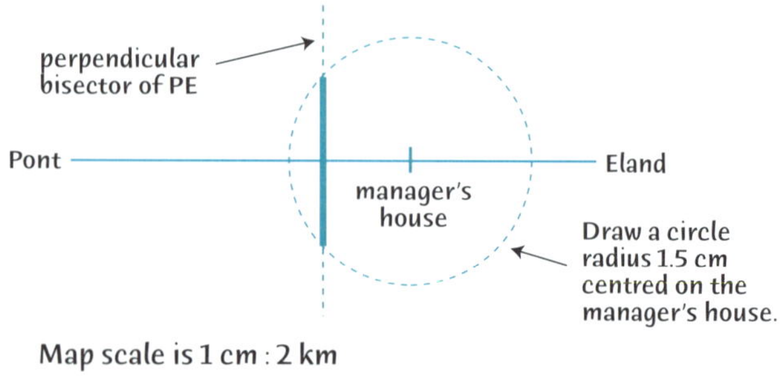

Key Facts and Skills

- the path of a point which stays at the **same distance from a given point** is a circle
- the path of a point which stays at the **same distance from two given points** is a straight line
- a straight line between two points may be **bisected** using ruler and compasses only
- **to construct a right angle**, draw a line and bisect it using ruler and compasses only

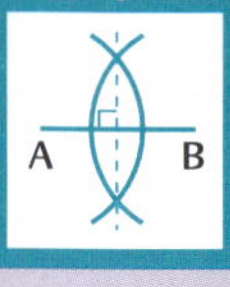

The Crash Course

Movement about one fixed straight line

The locus of a point which moves so that it is always the same distance from one given fixed straight line is a pair of parallel lines joined by two semi- (half) circles.

Movement about two fixed intersecting lines

The locus of a point which moves so that it is always the same distance from two given fixed intersecting lines is the pair of bisectors of the angles between the lines.

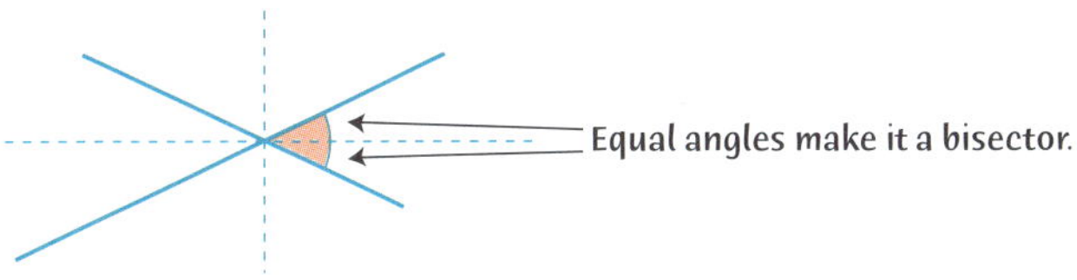

Steps for constructing the bisector of an angle

1 Open the compasses so the radius is about 2 cm.
2 With the compass point at the vertex P, draw an arc to cut the arms of the angle at X and Y.
3 With the compass point at X draw an arc.
4 With the compass point at Y, and using the same radius, draw another arc to intersect the previous one at Q.
5 Join P and Q, the point of intersection of the two arcs. This is the bisector of the angle P.

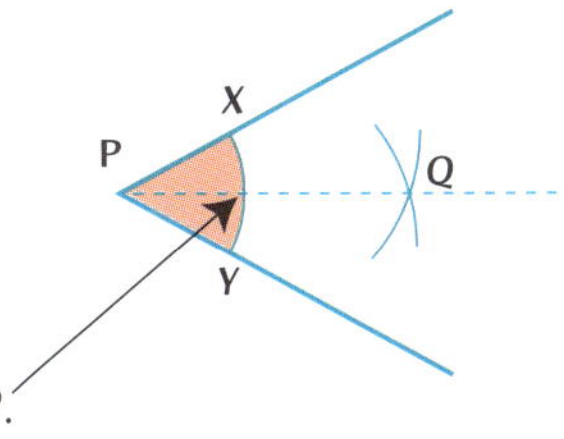

Tip: To construct an angle of 45°, bisect a right angle.

How to use loci to find positions

Loci can be used to solve problems involving positions and access.

Example

The fences between two gardens meet at an angle of 45°. Sam wants to plant a tree so that it is nearer his fence than his neighbour's. Shade the area where Sam may plant his tree.

- Construct an angle of 45°.
- Construct the bisector of the angle.
- Shade the area between Sam's fence and the bisector of the angle.

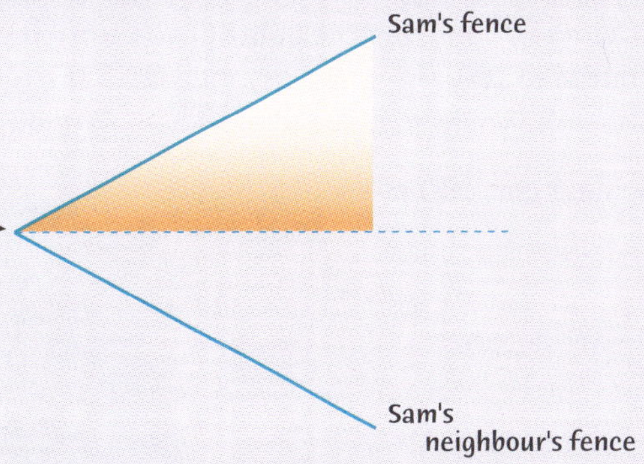

Key facts and skills

- the path of a point which stays the **same distance from a given straight line** is a pair of parallel lines joined at the ends by two semi-circles
- the path of a point which stays the **same distance from two given intersecting lines** is a pair of lines bisecting the angles between the lines
- to construct the **bisector of an angle**

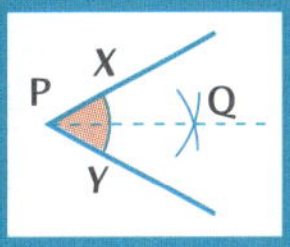

Exam Practice Questions

1 A yacht sails between two buoys A and B so that it stays the same distance from both of them. Keeping on the same path it then anchors so that it is 60 m from restaurant R. On the diagram, show the yacht's sailing path and where it anchors. Show your construction lines.

Scale: 1 cm : 40 m

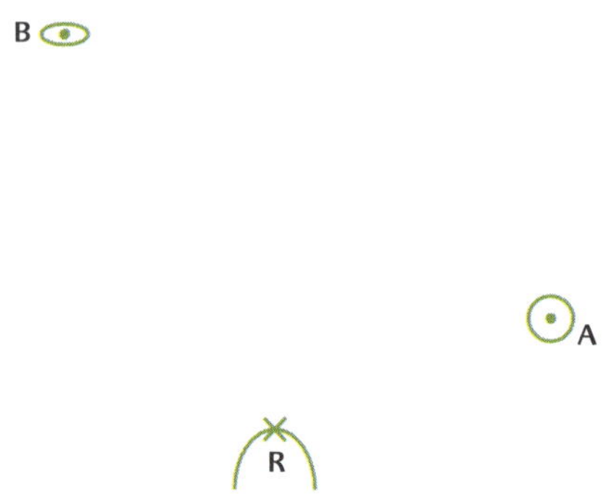

2 The bearing of Oxdon from Lonton is 45°. Oxdon is due east of Noron.
Using ruler and compasses only, draw a plan to show the position of Oxdon. Show your construction lines.

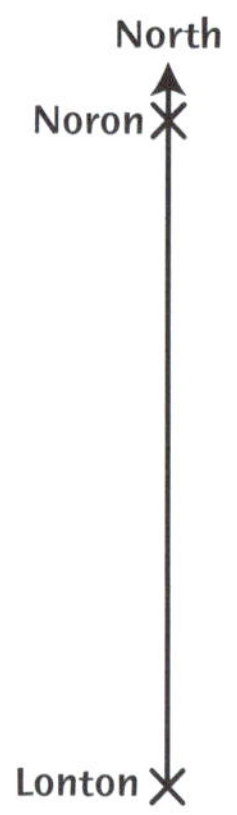

3 A yacht sails from A along a course so that it stays 100 m from the sea wall S. It then turns into the harbour, staying 100 m from the lighthouse L until it is the same distance from the sea walls S and W. Then it follows a course to stay the same distance from the two sea walls S and W. It anchors when it reaches shallow water. Show the yacht's path and mark where it anchors.

Scale: 1 cm : 100 m

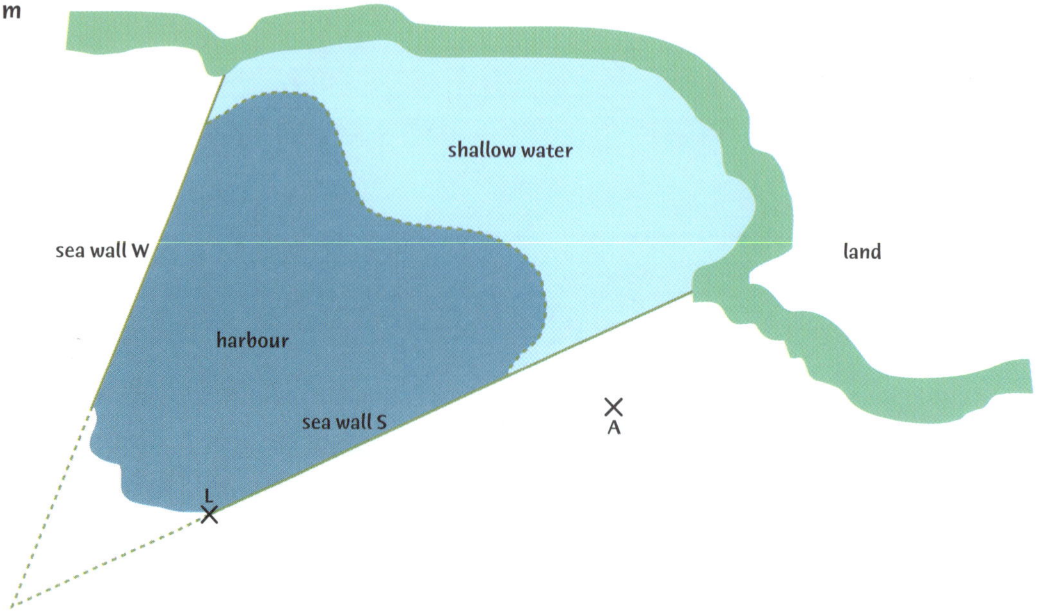

Revision Unit 15

Triangles

The Check Up

1 Find the value of x in this triangle.
Give your answer to 2 d.p.

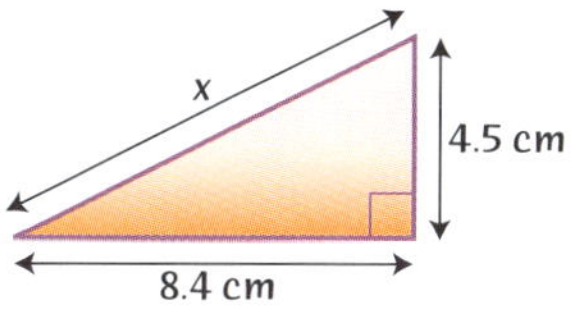

______

2 Find the value of y in this triangle.
Give your answer to 2 d.p.

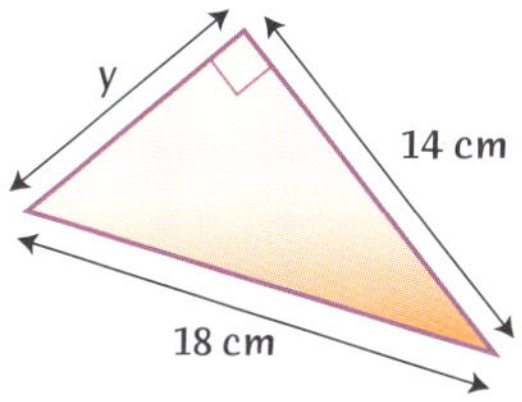

______

3 Is this triangle right-angled? Explain your answer.

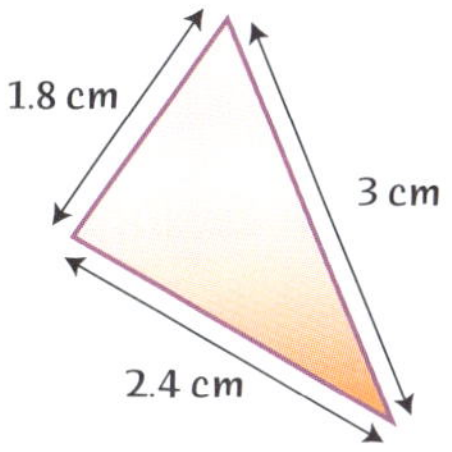

______

______

4 a) Show that triangles ABC and ADE are similar.

______

b) Find the length of BC.

______

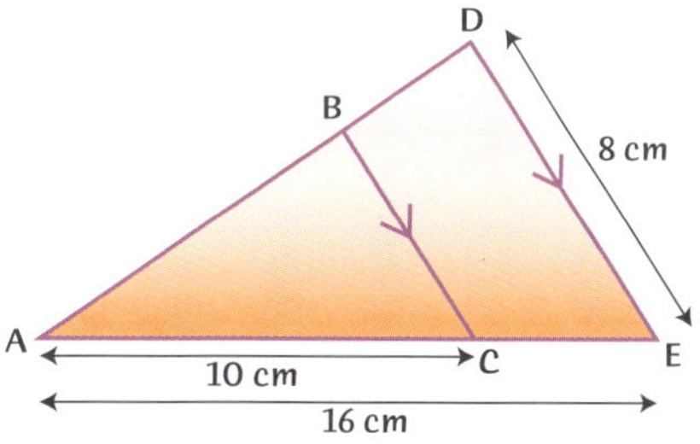

5 a) Show that the triangles XYZ and XVW are similar.

______

b) Find the length of YZ.

______

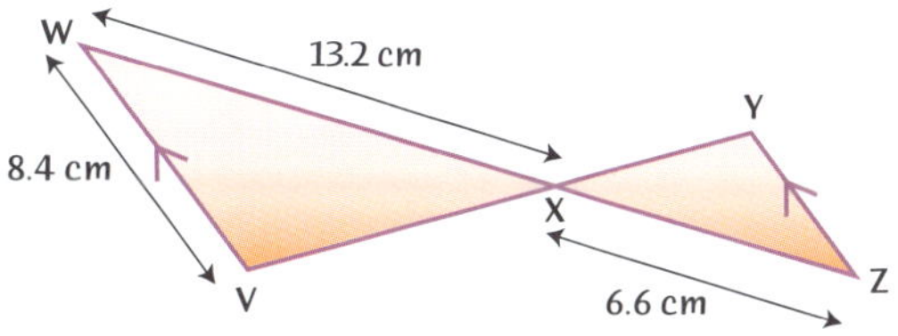

Mark yourself *(see answers on page 105)*

- Just a few wrong? You're geared up for the Exam Practice Questions. Go for it!
- More than a few wrong? Boost your learning powers by taking the Crash Course before you tackle the Exam Practice Questions.

/ 8

THE CRASH COURSE

Right-angled triangles

Pythagoras' theorem can be used to find missing lengths of sides in right-angled triangles.

Pythagoras' theorem

In this right-angled triangle:
$c^2 = a^2 + b^2$
where c is the **hypotenuse** (the side opposite the right angle).

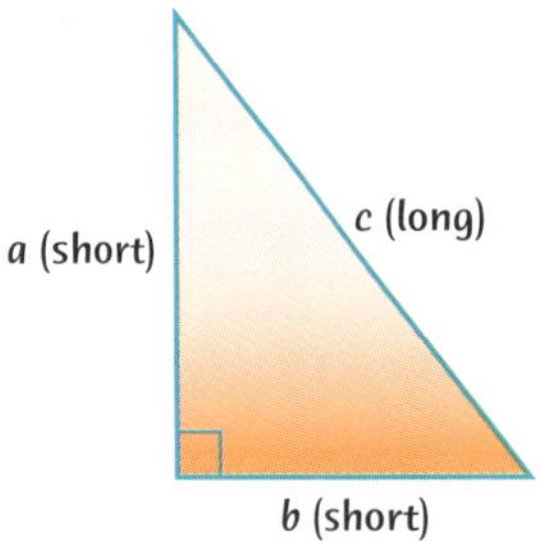

Tip:

Remember:
$(\text{longside})^2 = (\text{shortside})^2 + (\text{shortside})^2$
$(\text{shortside})^2 = (\text{longside})^2 - (\text{shortside})^2$

Steps for finding the length of a side using Pythagoras' theorem

A ladder is 4 m long. The ladder can't be placed nearer than 1.2 m horizontally from a vertical wall. The bottom of Tom's bedroom window is 3.9 m from the ground. Could he climb in? Explain your answer.

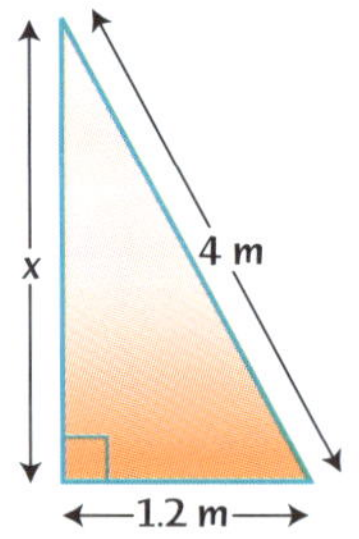

1. Draw the correct right-angled triangle.
2. Label the side you want, which is the height Tom can reach with the ladder, x.
3. Square the sides you know:
   $4^2 = 16$
   $1.2^2 = 1.44$
4. You want a short side, so subtract.
   $x^2 = 16 - 1.44 = 14.56$
5. Take the square root of 14.56 to find x.
   $x = \sqrt{14.56} = 3.8$ m (1 d.p.)

   As the window is 3.9 m high, if Tom is agile he should be to able climb in.

How to use Pythagoras' theorem to show that a triangle is right-angled

If Pythagoras' theorem is true for the sides of a triangle, then the triangle is right-angled.

EXAMPLE

Zara has constructed a right-angled triangle, but her teacher says that it doesn't look correct. She measures the sides of the triangle and gets 4.8 cm, 6.4 cm and 8.0 cm. Has she drawn the triangle accurately??

- Square the sides: $4.8^2 = 23.04$, $6.4^2 = 40.96$, $8.0^2 = 64.0$
- Add the squares of the two short sides: $23.04 + 40.96 = 64.0$
  $(\text{shortside})^2 + (\text{shortside})^2 = (\text{longside})^2$
  This agrees with Pythagoras' theorem so Zara's triangle is correct.

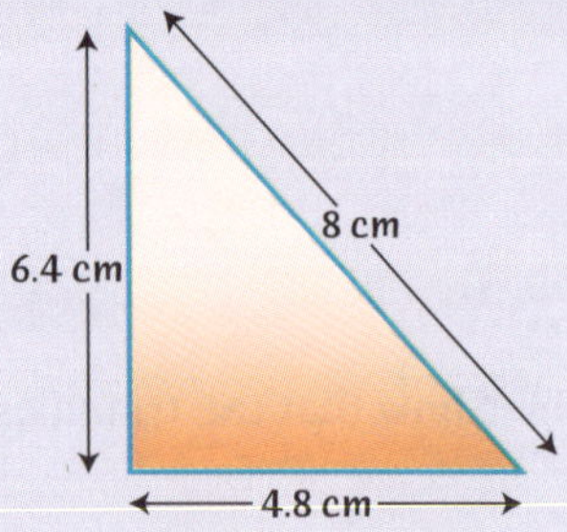

KEY FACTS AND SKILLS

- use **Pythagoras' theorem** in right-angled triangles
- $(\text{shortside})^2 = (\text{longside})^2 - (\text{shortside})^2$
  $(\text{longside})^2 = (\text{shortside})^2 + (\text{shortside})^2$
- if **Pythagoras' theorem** is true for the sides of a triangle, it is **right-angled**

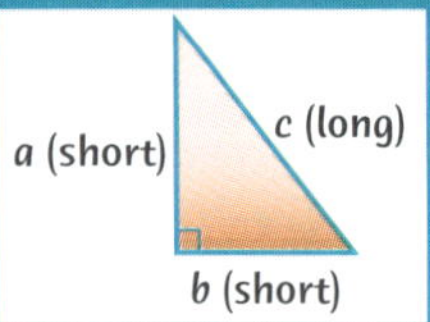

THE CRASH COURSE

Similar triangles

If two triangles are **similar**, the **angles** in one triangle **are equal to** the angles in the other, and their **corresponding sides** are in the same ratio. In triangles ABC and DE, $\angle A = \angle D$, $\angle B = \angle E$, $\angle C = \angle F$ so the triangles are similar.

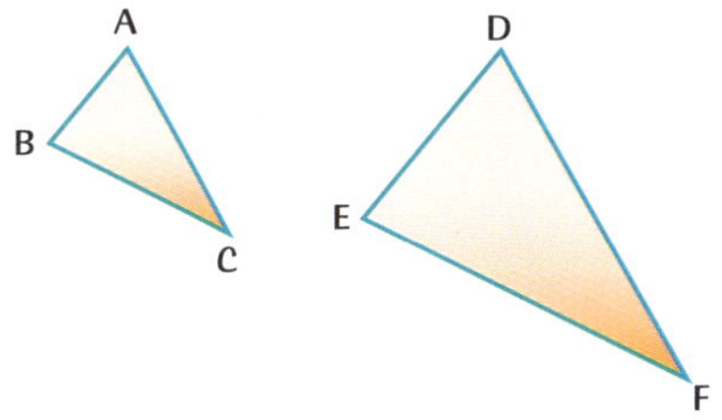

It follows that $\frac{AB}{DE} = \frac{BC}{EF} = \frac{AC}{DF}$ or in ratio form AB : DE = BC : EF = AC : DF

Tip: Draw similar triangles so that the equal angles are in the same relative positions.

Steps for finding the length of a side using similar triangles

In the diagram BC is parallel to DE.
AB = 1.5 m, BC = 1.2 m and AD = 3.5 m.
Find DE.

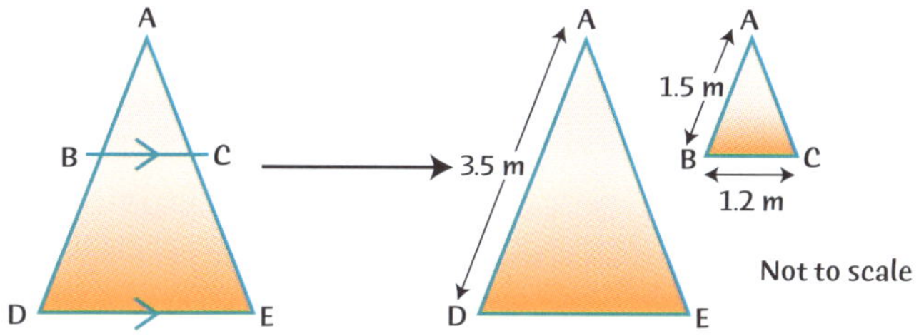

1. Show that the triangles are similar.
   $\angle ADE = \angle ABC$ (corresponding angles)
   $\angle AED = \angle ACB$ (corresponding angles)
   $\angle BAC$ is common to both triangles
2. Separate the similar triangles and use the ratios of corresponding sides.
   $\frac{DE}{BC} = \frac{AD}{AB}$ so $\frac{DE}{1.2} = \frac{3.5}{1.5}$
3. Solve the equation.
   Multiply both sides by 1.2. $DE = \frac{3.5 \times 1.2}{1.5} = 2.8$ m

EXAMPLE

In the figure BA is 3.1 cm, AC is 2.3 cm and DC is 1.5 cm. AB and DE are horizontal.
Find DE.

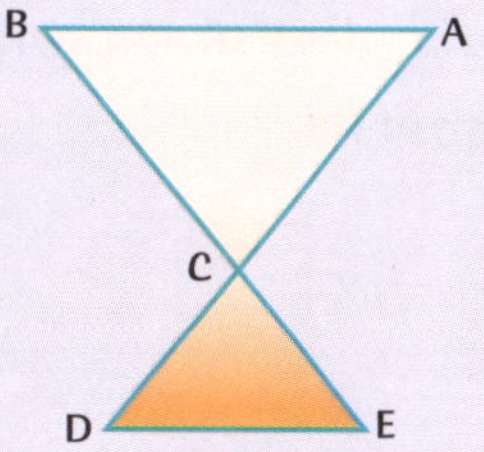

1. Show that the triangles are similar.
   AB is parallel to DE so
   $\angle CDE = \angle CAB$ (alternate angles)
   $\angle CED = \angle CBA$ (alternate angles)
   $\angle BCA = \angle ECD$ (vertically opposite angles)
   So the triangles are similar.
2. Separate the similar triangles and use the ratio formulae.
   $\frac{DE}{AB} = \frac{DC}{AC}$ so $\frac{DE}{3.1} = \frac{1.5}{2.3}$
3. Solve the equation.
   Multiply both sides by 3.1. $DE = \frac{1.5 \times 3.1}{2.3} = 2.0$ cm (1 d.p.)

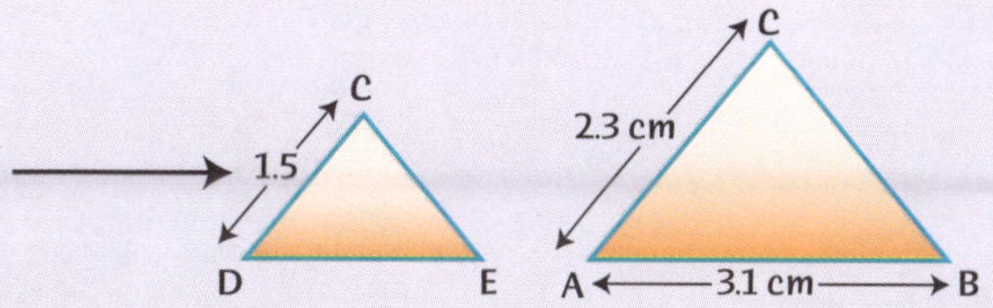

KEY FACTS AND SKILLS

- **similar triangles** have equal angles
- **corresponding sides in similar triangles** are in the same ratio

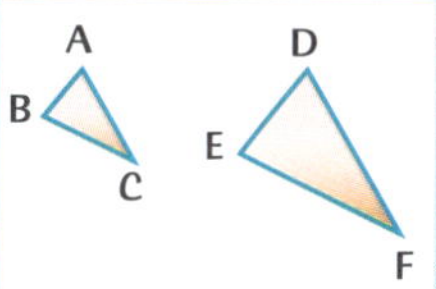

Exam Practice Questions

1 A boats starts at A and sails 15.5 km due east to B, then turns and sails 9.1 km due north to C. Draw a diagram and work out AC, which is how far the boat is from its starting position. Give your answer correct to 1 d.p.

2 a) Find the length of CD.

b) Find the length of BD.

Give your answers correct to 2 d.p.

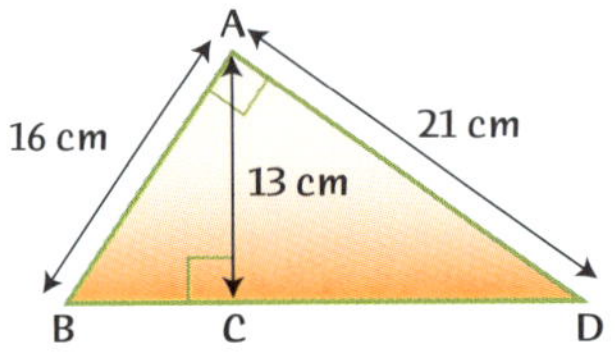

3 a) Calculate the size of $\angle QSR$. Explain your answer.

b) Using similar triangles:

(i) calculate the length of PR

(ii) calculate the length of SR.

Give your answers correct to 2 d.p.

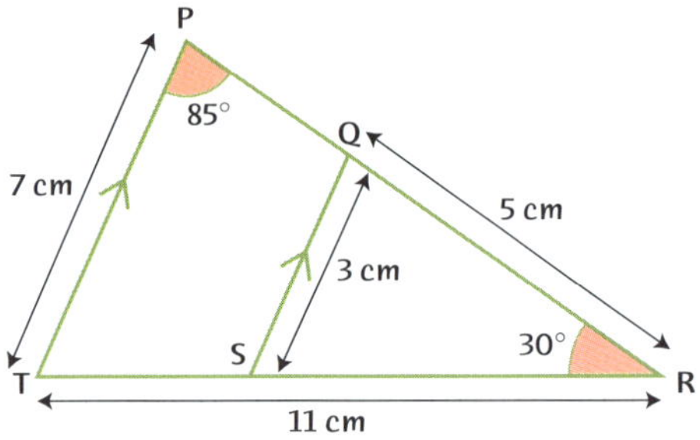

4 In the figure AC : BC = 5 : 1.

a) Use similar triangles to find the length of AE.

b) Work out the length of ED.

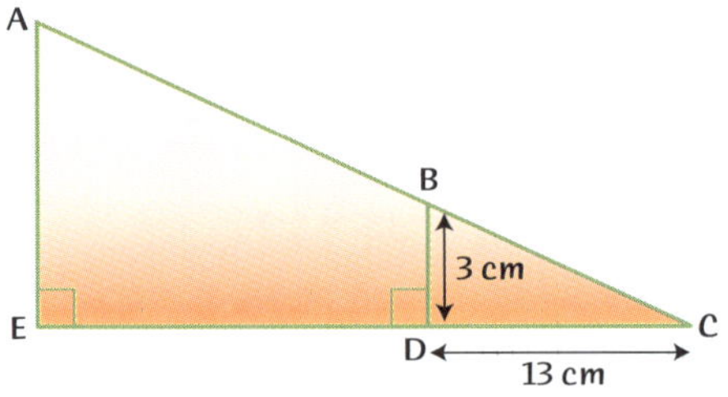

5 a) Explain why triangles PSR and SQR are similar.

b) Find the length of PR.

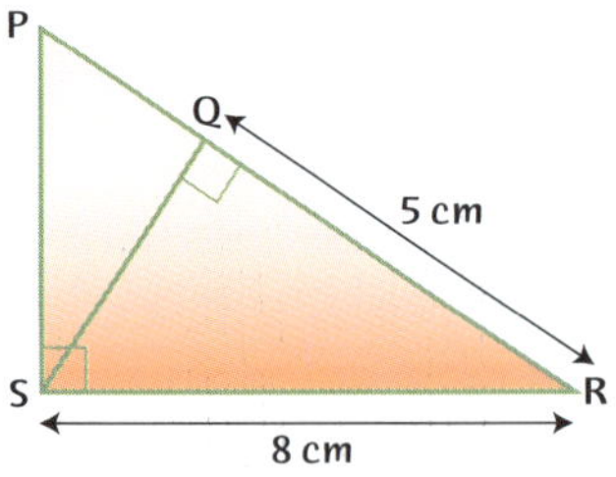

Revision Unit 16

Trigonometry

The Check Up

1 Find the value of x in the figure.
Give your answer correct to 1 d.p.

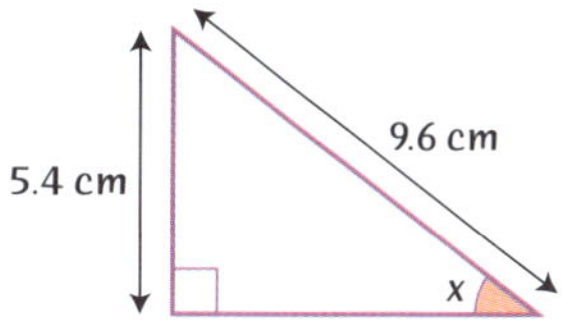

2 Find the length of the side y in the triangle.
Give your answer correct to 2 d.p.

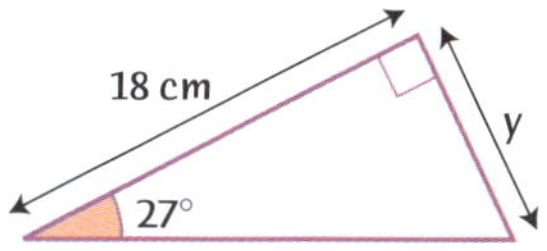

3 Find the value of z in the figure.
Give your answer correct to 3 s.f.

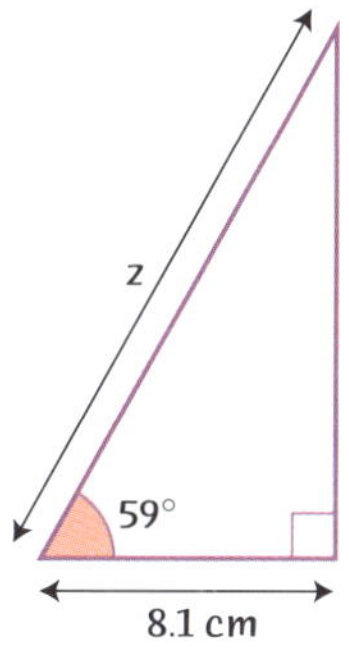

4 Find the value of w in the figure.
Give your answer correct to 2 d.p.

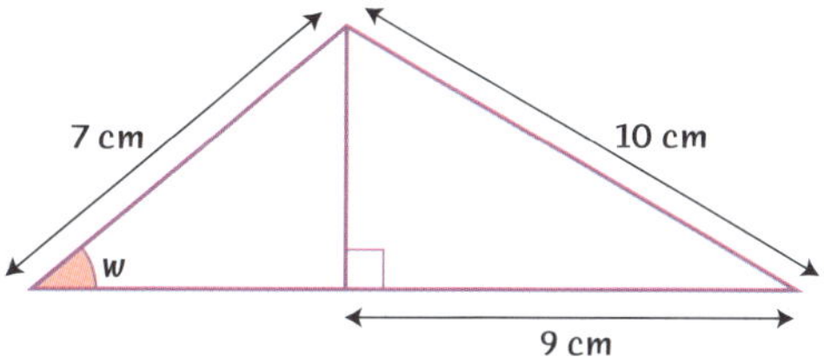

Mark yourself *(see answers on page 105)*

- Just a few wrong? You're geared up for the Exam Practice Questions. Go for it!
- More than a few wrong? Boost your learning powers by taking the Crash Course before you tackle the Exam Practice Questions.

/4

THE CRASH COURSE

Definitions

In any right-angled triangle the three trigonometric ratios sine(sin), cosine (cos) and tangent (tan) are defined as:

$\sin x = \frac{o}{h}$ $\cos x = \frac{a}{h}$ $\tan x = \frac{o}{a}$

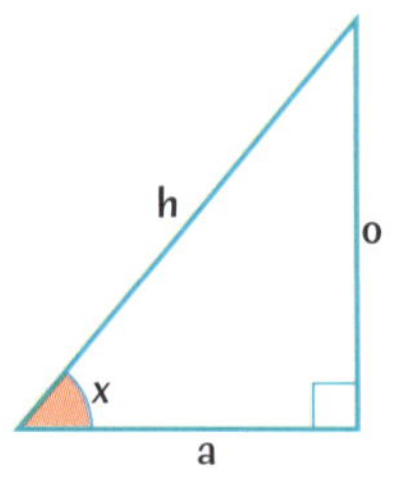

o is the side opposite the angle
a is the side adjacent (next to) the angle
h is the hypotenuse (opposite the right angle).
The trigonometric ratios can be used to find angles and sides in right-angled triangles.

Tip: Remember: soh cah toa

How to find the size of an angle

In a right-angled triangle, if two sides are known then the trigonometric ratios can be used to find the sizes of the other two angles.

Steps for finding the size of an angle if you have two sides

Find the value of z in the figure.

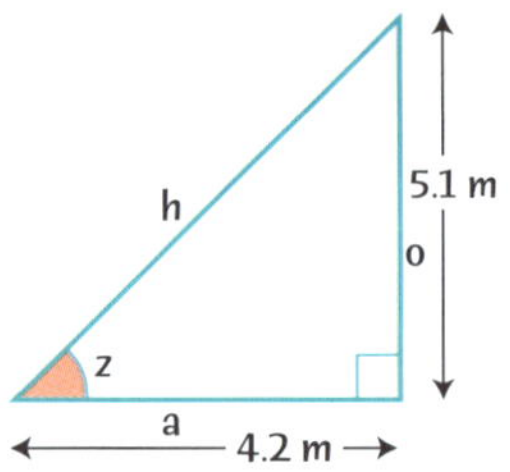

1 Label the sides o, a and h: o = 5.1, a = 4.2
2 Choose the correct trigonometric ratio: you have o and a, use tan.
3 Use the ratio to make the equation: $\tan z = \frac{o}{a} = \frac{5.1}{4.2}$
4 Find the angle using your calculator. $z = 50.5°$

To use the calculator, key: 5 · 1 ÷ 4 · 2 = shift tan

The calculator displays the answer: 50.5

Remember to check the instructions for your own calculator.

Tip: Make sure your calculator is operating in degrees.

KEY FACTS AND SKILLS

- **label the sides** of a right-angled triangle, o is **opposite**, a is **adjacent**, h is **hypotenuse**
- the **trigonometric ratios** are $\sin x = \frac{o}{h}$, $\cos x = \frac{a}{h}$, $\tan x = \frac{o}{a}$
- **to find an angle**, label the sides o, a and h and choose the ratio using what you know to find what you want
- **use the ratio** to make an equation
- **use the shift/second function calculator key**

THE CRASH COURSE

How to find the length of a side

In a right-angled triangle, if one angle and one side are given, then the trigonometric ratios can be used to find the lengths of the other two sides.

Steps for finding the length of a side, given one side and one angle

Find the value of y *in the figure*.

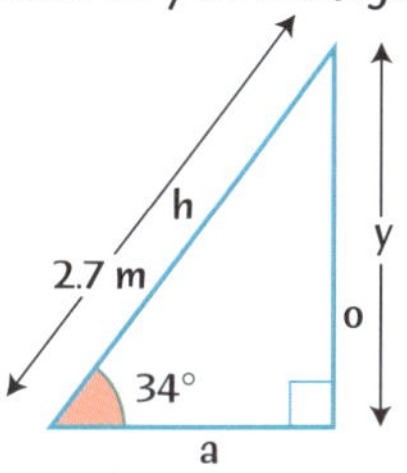

1 Label the sides o, a and h: $o = y, h = 2.7$

2 Choose the correct ratio: you have h, you want o, use sin.

3 Make the equation: $\sin 34^\circ = \frac{o}{h} = \frac{y}{2.7}$

4 Use your calculator to find the sin of the angle: $\sin 34^\circ = 0.559$

To use your calculator, key: **3** **4** **sin**

Check your own calculator.

The calculator displays the answer: 0.559

5 Solve the equation: $0.559 = \frac{y}{2.7}$ ← y up here so multiply by the trigonometric ratio

6 Multiply both sides by 2.7: $y = 2.7 \times 0.559 = 1.51$ m (2 d.p.)

When the required value is in the denominator

Take care when the value you want appears in the denominator. Divide the given side by the trigonometric ratio.

Steps for finding the length of the hypotenuse, given one side and one angle

Find the value of y *in the figure*.

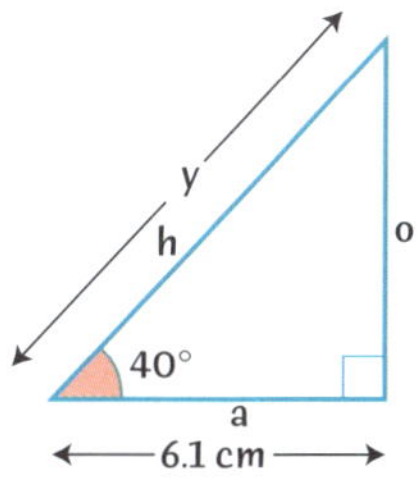

1 Label the sides o, a and h: $h = y, a = 6.1$

2 Choose the correct ratio: you have a, you want h, use cos.

3 Use the ratio to make an equation: $\cos 40^\circ = \frac{a}{h} = \frac{6.1}{y}$

4 Use a calculator to find the value of the ratio: $\cos 40^\circ = 0.766$

5 Solve the equation (Take care!): $0.766 = \frac{6.1}{y}$ ← y down here so divide by the trigonometric ratio

$0.766 \times y = 6.1$

7 Divide both sides by 0.766: $y = 6.1 \div 0.766 = 7.96$ cm (2 d.p.)

KEY FACTS AND SKILLS

- **to find a side**, label the sides o, a and h and choose the ratio for what you know
- **use the ratio** to make an equation
- **use a calculator** to find the value of the selected ratio
- **to solve the equation**, multiply the known side by the value of the ratio
- **if the value you want is in the denominator**, divide the known side by the value of the ratio

Exam Practice Questions

1 The point X is 1.4 m from the base of the lamp post. The angle of elevation of the top of the lamp post from X is 61°. How high is the lamp post?
Give your answer correct to 2 d.p.

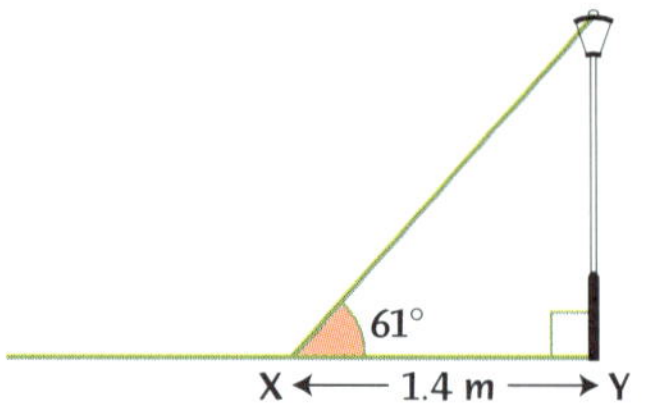

2 A ladder is 12 feet long and must be placed no more than 9 feet from the wall. What size is the angle the ladder makes with the horizontal ground?
Give your answer correct to 1 d.p.

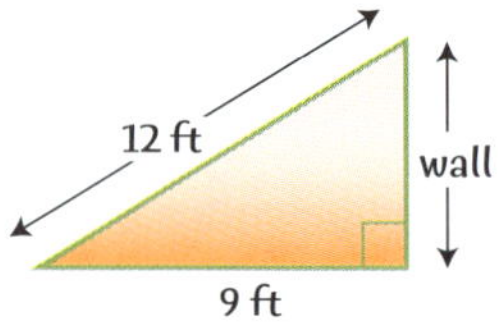

3 Camford is 134 km due west of Lonbridge. Lonbridge is 118 km due north of Shefford.
What is the bearing of Camford from Shefford?
Give your answer correct to 1 d.p.

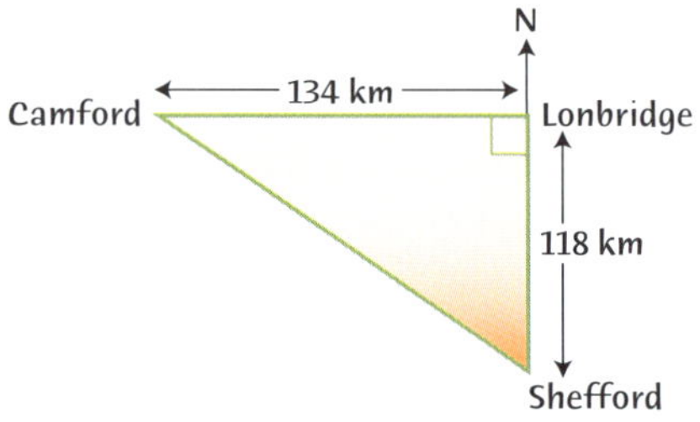

4 The figure represents a bridge over a small stream. The first ramp AH is 4.5 m long and makes an angle of 15° with the horizontal ground. The horizontal portion of the bridge HV is 3.5 m long and the second ramp VB is 3 m long. Give your answers to a suitable degree of accuracy.

a) Calculate AS, the distance from the start of the bridge to the stream.

b) Calculate the height HS of the bridge over the stream.

c) Calculate the angle x which the second ramp makes with the ground.

d) Find the length of AB.

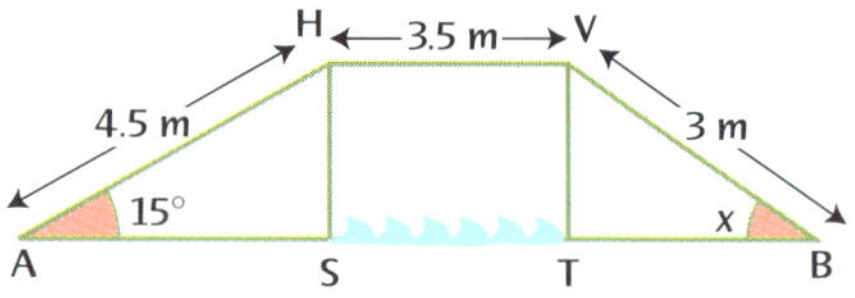

5 From U the angle of depression of V is 17° and the angle of depression of W is 41°.
The height UX of U from the horizontal ground is 8 m.

a) Calculate WX.

b) Calculate VW.

Give your answers correct to 2 s.f.

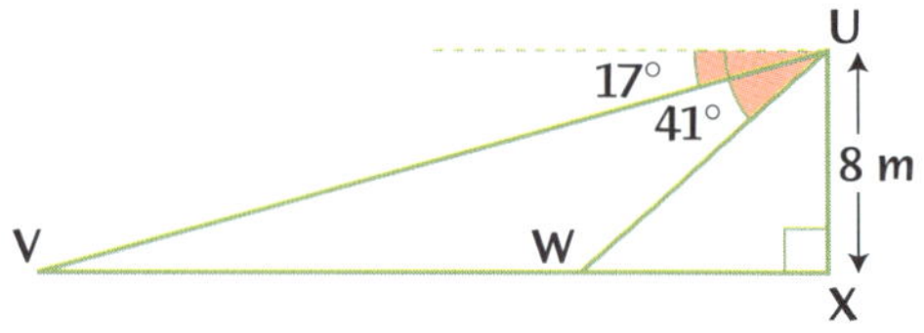

Revision Unit 11

Length and Area

The Check Up

1 Find the perimeter of this shape which is a quarter of a circle, radius 4 cm. Give your answer to 1 d.p.

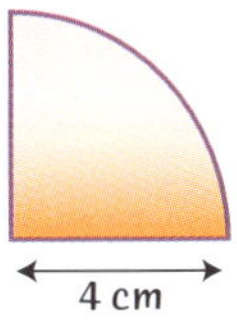

____

2 A car wheel has diameter 57 cm.
How many complete revolutions does it make when the car travels a distance of 1 km? _______________

3 a) Find the perimeter of this shape.

____

b) Find its area.

____

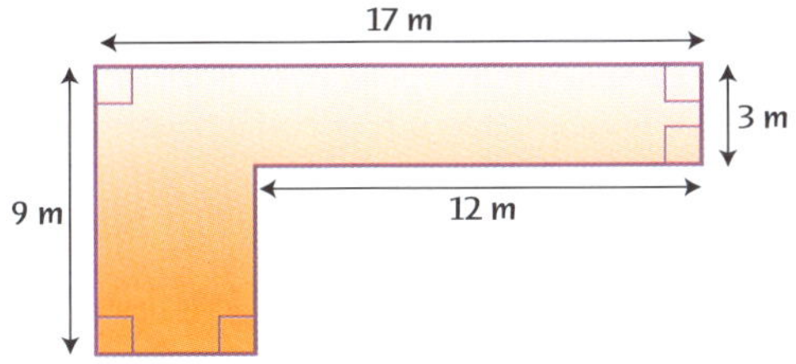

4 Find the area of each of these shapes.

a) a semi-circle, diameter 5 inches

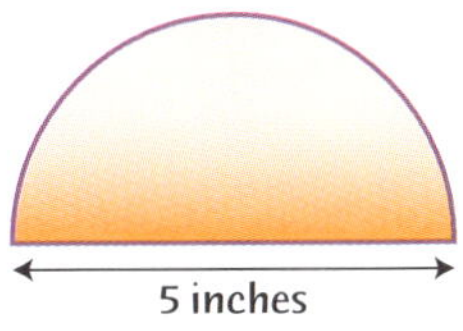

____

b) a rhombus, length of side 3 cm and height 2.5 cm

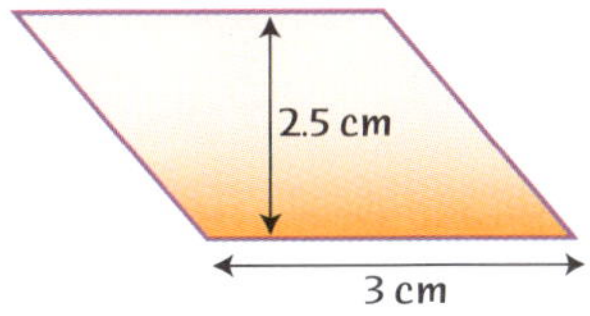

____

c) a right-angled triangle with sides of length 5 m and 4.5 m, as shown.

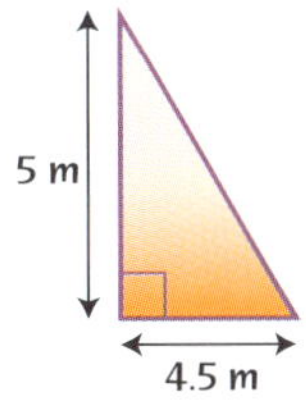

____

Give your answers correct to 1 d.p.

5 Find the area of the side elevation of this hut, with dimensions as shown. Give your answer correct to 1 d.p.

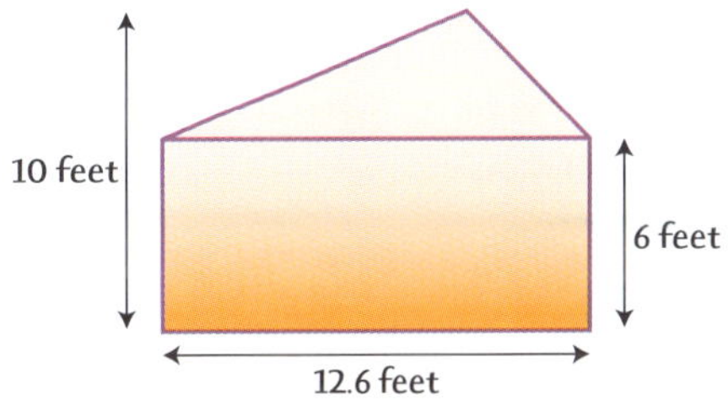

____

Mark yourself *(see answers on page 106)*

- **Just a few wrong?** You're geared up for the Exam Practice Questions. Go for it!
- **More than a few wrong?** Boost your learning powers by taking the Crash Course before you tackle the Exam Practice Questions.

/ 8

THE CRASH COURSE

Length

The **perimeter** of a plane (flat) figure is the distance all the way round the figure.
It is measured in length units such as metres (m), centimetres (cm), millimetres (mm).
The perimeter of a circle is called the **circumference**.
The circumference of this circle is $\pi \times d$
π is a number approximately equal to 3.142.
In calculations involving π use the π key on the calculator.

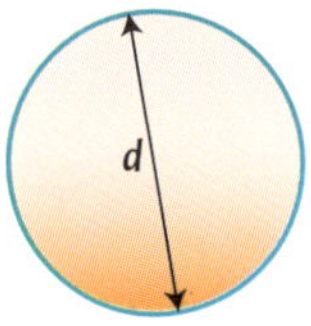

How to find the perimeters of shapes

To find the perimeter, start at one point and go round, adding the sides, until you come back to the beginning.

EXAMPLE

Find the perimeter of this race track.
The track has two semi-circular ends of diameter 70 m joined by two straight sections of length 90 m.

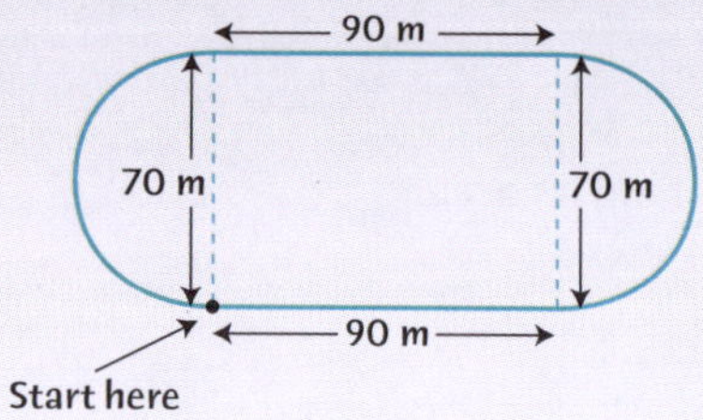

The perimeter is 90 + half circumference + 90 + half circumference
= 180 + circumference
The circumference is $\pi \times 70 = 219.9$ m
The perimeter of the track is 180 + 219.9 = 400 m (3 s.f.)

How to use the circumference formula 'the other way round'!

The circumference of a circular tree is 0.96 m. What is the diameter of the tree?

- The circumference is $\pi \times d = 0.96$ m
- So $d = 0.96 \div \pi = 0.31$ m (2 d.p.)

Tip: When a wheel makes one revolution, a point on its rim travels a distance of one circumference.

Area

The area of a plane figure is the amount of flat space it takes up. It is measured in square units such as square metres (m^2), square centimetres (cm^2), square millimetres (mm^2).

Area of an irregular shape

Draw a grid and count the approximate number of squares the shape occupies.
To find the area of this leaf, draw a centimetre grid and count the squares.
The area of the leaf is approximately 2 cm^2.

Area of a square is (length of side)^2

Area of this square is a^2.

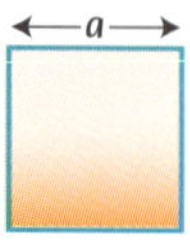

Area of a rectangle is length $\times$ width

Area of this rectangle is $a \times b$.

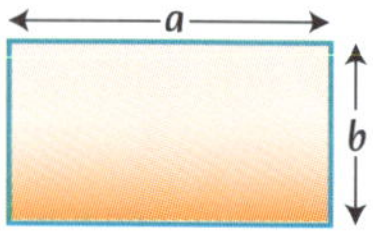

Area of a circle is $\pi \times (\text{radius})^2$

Area of this circle is $\pi \times r^2$.

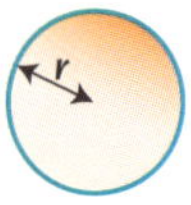

How to use the formula for the area of a circle 'the other way round'

If the area of a circular pond is 21 m^2, what is its radius?

- Area = $\pi \times r^2 = 21$ m^2 and $r^2 = 21 \div \pi = 4.58$ m^2
- $r = \sqrt{4.58} = 2.1$ m (1 d.p.)

THE CRASH COURSE

Area of a triangle is half base × height

The area of each of these triangles is $\frac{1}{2} \times b \times h$.

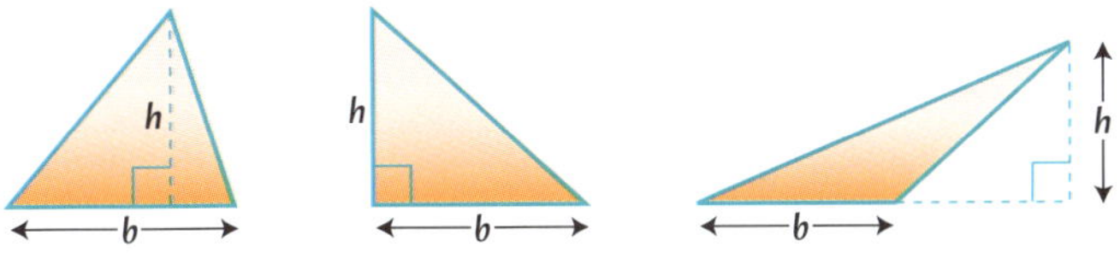

Area of a parallelogram is base × height

A parallelogram looks like a rectangle that has been pushed over.
The area of this parallelogram is $b \times h$.

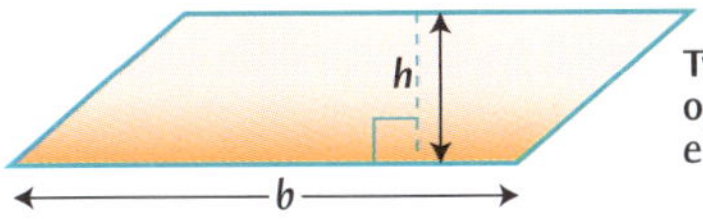

Two pairs of opposite sides equal and parallel

Area of a rhombus is base × height

A rhombus looks like a square that has been pushed over.
The area of this rhombus is $b \times h$.

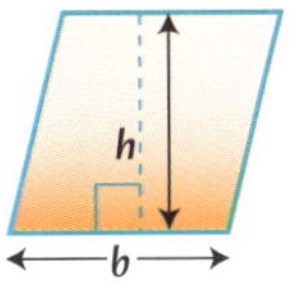

A parallelogram with equal sides

Area of a trapezium is half height × sum of parallel sides

The area of this trapezium is $\frac{1}{2} \times h \times (a + b)$.

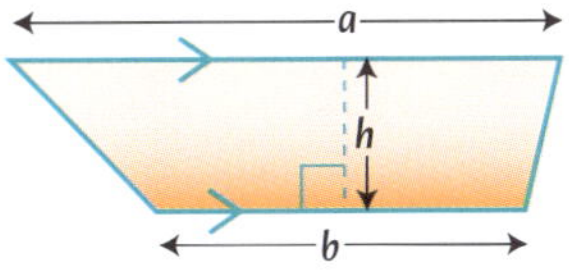

One pair of opposite sides parallel.

Working with area formulae

Triangles AED, BED and CED all have equal areas.
Each triangle has:

- the same base (DE)
- the same height (h).

The area of a triangle is $\frac{1}{2} \times b \times h$ so the triangles must have equal areas.

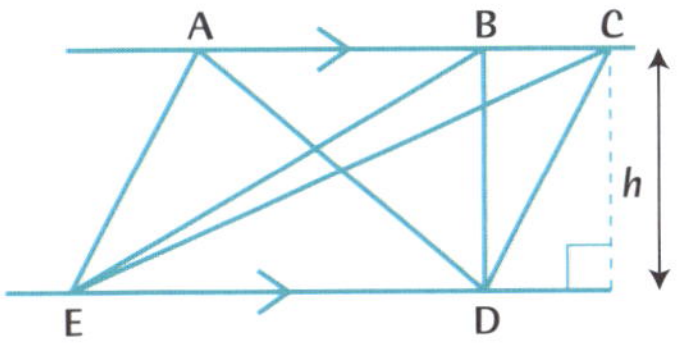

Tip: Because area involves two dimensions, it is important to use the same unit of length for each. Do not mix units, for example m with cm.

Finding the areas of complicated shapes

To find the area of a complicated shape, divide it up into simple shapes with areas that are easier to find.
Find the area of this door by separating it into a rectangle and a semi-circle.

 you separate it into:  a rectangle and  a semi-circle.

A **kite** has two pairs of adjacent sides (next to each other) equal.
To find its area divide it into isosceles triangles.

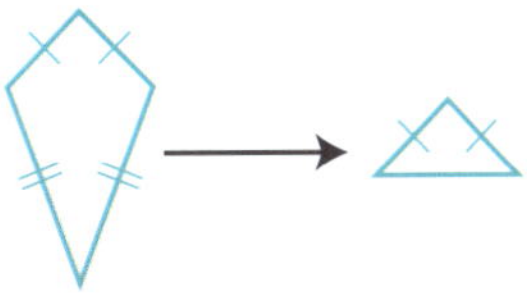 and 

KEY FACTS AND SKILLS

- the **perimeter** is the distance all the way round a figure
- the **circumference** of a circle is $\pi \times$ diameter
- the **area of a square** is (length of side)^2
- the **area of a rectangle** is length × breadth
- the **area of a circle** is $\pi \times$ (radius)^2
- the **area of a triangle** is half base × height
- the **area of a parallelogram** is base × height; the **area of a rhombus** is base × height
- the **area of a trapezium** is half height × sum of the parallel sides

EXAM PRACTICE QUESTIONS

1 Find:

a) the area of this shape

b) the perimeter of this shape.

(Use Pythagoras' theorem to find x.)

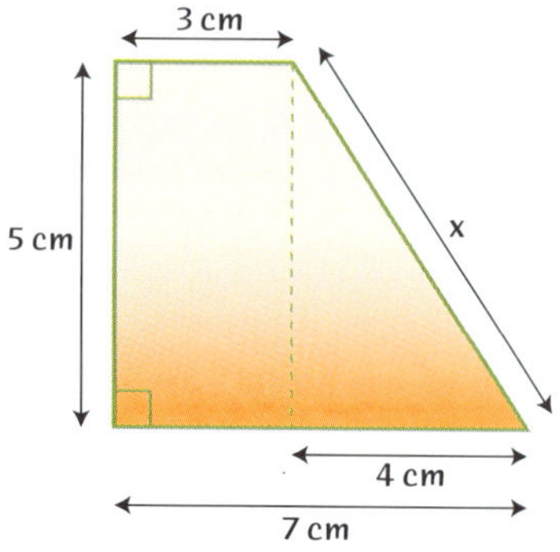

2 A scoreboard is made of three circles with the same centre.
The radius of the outside circle is 20 cm, the radius of the next circle is 15 cm and the inner circle has an area of 200 cm^2.

a) Find the radius of the inner circle. Give your answer correct to 1 d.p.

b) Find the area of the outer ring. Give your answer correct to the nearest whole number.

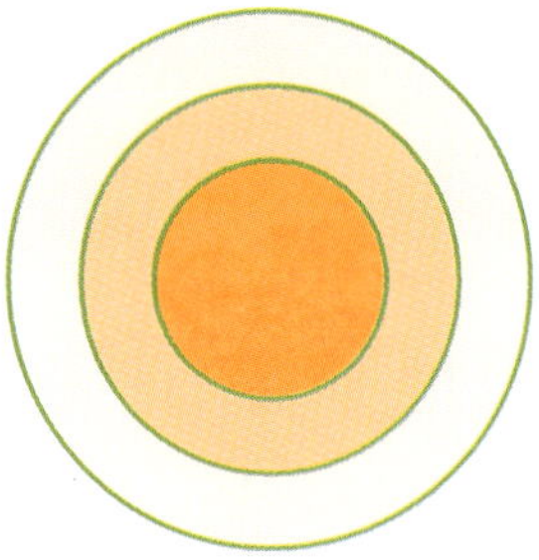

3 a) What is the perimeter of this parallelogram?

b) Work out its area.

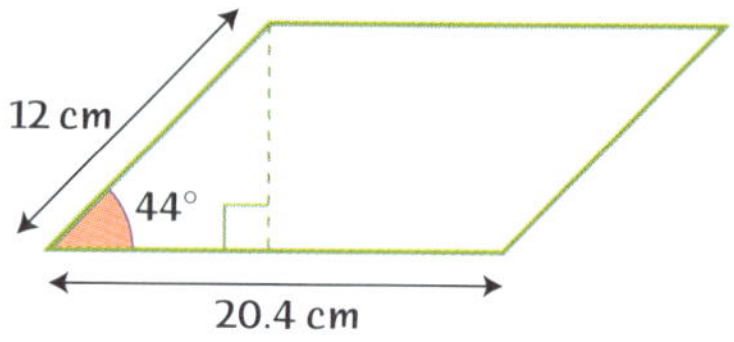

4 A lawn is in the shape of a semi-circle of diameter 12 m.

a) Find the perimeter of the lawn.

b) The gardener plans to plant pansies completely round the lawn.
If one plant is put in every 20 cm, how many plants will be needed?

c) Find the area of the lawn.

d) The lawn needs fertiliser. If one box is enough for 14 m^2, how many boxes are needed?

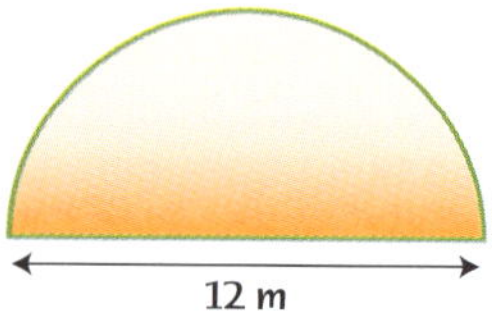

5 A road sign is in the shape of a triangle as shown.

a) What is the area of the sign?

The sign indicates cross-roads, and has the dimensions shown.

b) What is the area of the green cross?

c) What is the area of surrounding white?

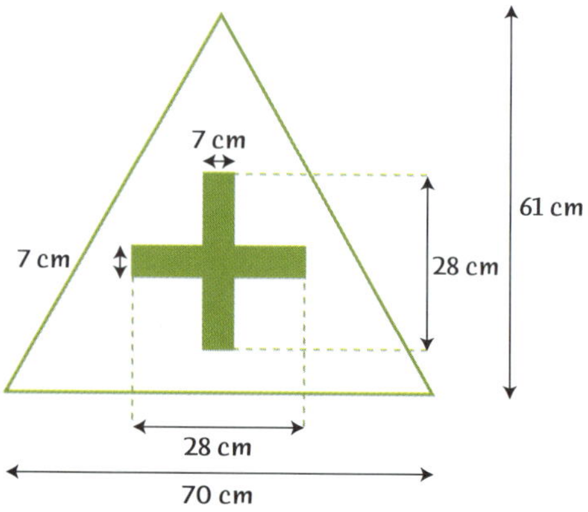

Revision Unit 18

3D shapes

The Check Up

1 A tank is a cuboid with dimensions 1.2 m by 2 m by 2.5 m.

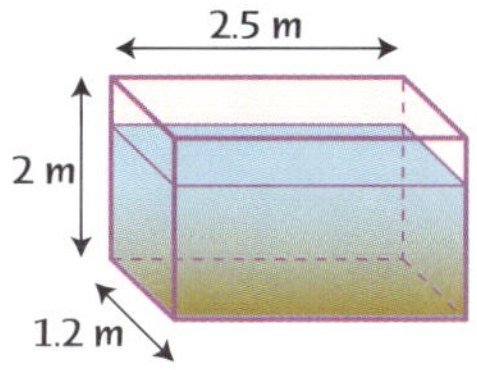

a) What is the volume of the tank? ____________

b) The tank contains water to a depth of 1.5 m.
Find the volume of water. Give your answer in litres. ____________

2 This is the net of a triangular prism with dimensions as shown.
Calculate c and then find the volume of the prism.

____

____

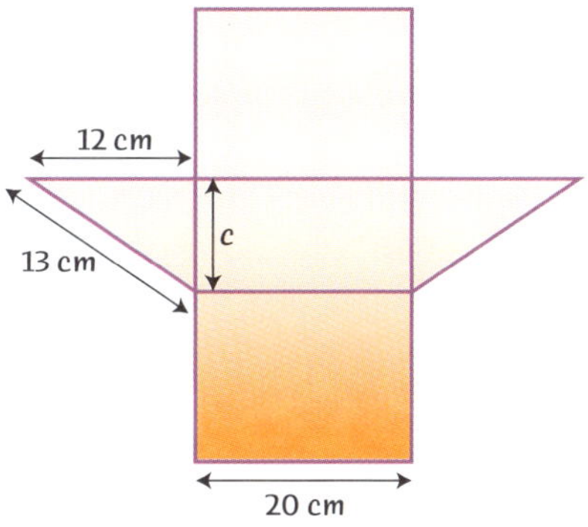

3 A cylindrical mug has internal diameter of 8 cm and internal height of 8.5 cm.

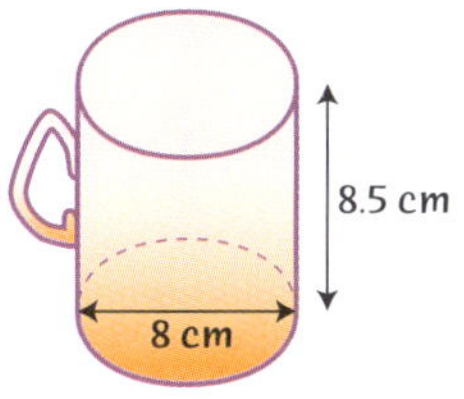

a) Calculate the maximum volume of tea the mug can hold.

Give you answer in litres, correct to 3 d.p. ____________

b) A tea urn holds 20 litres. How many complete

mugs of tea can be filled from the full urn? ____________

4 A cube has sides of length 3 cm. What is the surface area of the cube? ____________

5 A cylinder has internal radius 5 cm and capacity 2450 millilitres.
What is the internal height of the cylinder? Give your answer to the nearest centimetre. ____________

6 In the following expressions the letters d, e, f and g represent lengths.

a) gde ____________

b) $4\pi f^2$ ____________

c) $2(de + eg + gd)$ ____________

d) $g^2 + d^2$ ____________

e) $\frac{g^2}{e}$ ____________

f) $\frac{4}{3}\pi f^3$ ____________

Identify whether each expression measures length, area or volume.

Mark yourself *(see answers on page 106)*

- Just a few wrong? You're geared up for the Exam Practice Questions. Go for it!
- More than a few wrong? Boost your learning powers by taking the Crash Course before you tackle the Exam Practice Questions.

/ 14

The Crash Course

Three-dimensional shapes

The volume of a 3D shape is the amount of space it takes up. It is measured in cubic units such as cubic metres (m^3), cubic centimetres (cm^3) or cubic millimetres (mm^3).

This is a tetrahedron. It has:

- 4 triangular faces (flat surfaces)
- 4 vertices (points or corners)
- 6 edges (straight lines).

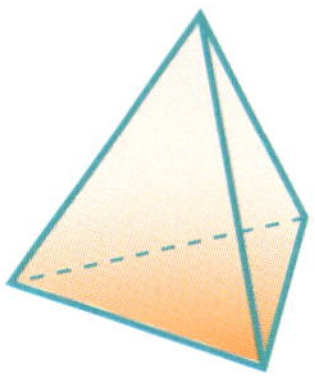

Nets

If a hollow 3D shape is cut along its edges and then flattened, the 2D shape formed is the net of the solid.

Cubes

A cube has all its sides of equal length. All its faces are squares. Ordinary dice are cubes.
The volume of a cube is length × length × length.
The volume of this cube is a^3.

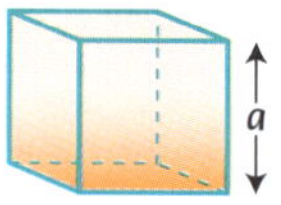

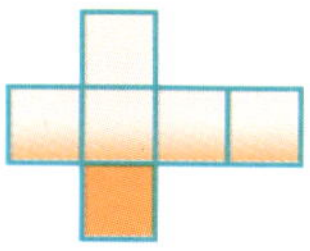
Net of a cube

Cuboids

A cuboid does not have all its sides equal. All its faces are rectangles. Bricks and shoe boxes are cuboids.
The volume of a cuboid is length × width × height.
The volume of this cuboid is $a \times b \times c$.

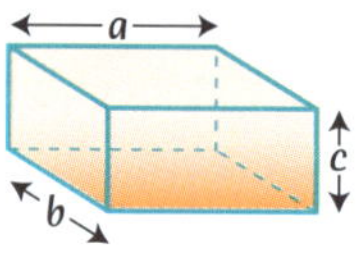

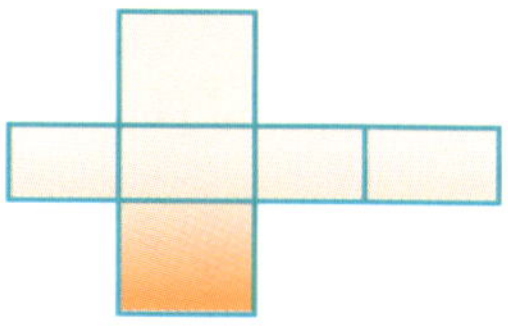
Net of a cuboid

Prisms

A prism is a shape with a constant cross-section. Toblerone bars and girders are prisms.
The volume of a prism is area of cross-section × length.
The volume of this prism is $A \times l$.

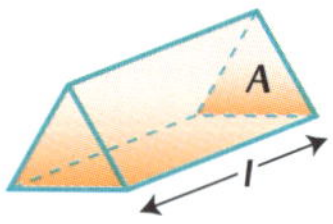

Net of a prism

Cylinders

A cylinder is a prism with circular cross-section. A can of cola is a cylinder.
The volume of a cylinder is area of base × height.
The volume of this cylinder is $\pi \times r^2 \times h$.

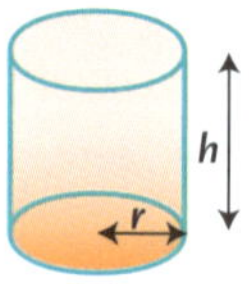

Net of a cylinder

Working with volume formulae

Example

A cylindrical can of soup has a base of radius 3.5 cm. The volume of the can is 400 cm^3.
What is the height of the can?

- Let the height be h cm.
- The volume of the can is $\pi \times r^2 \times h = 400$ cm^3.
- $\pi \times 3.5^2 \times h = 400$
  $38.48 \times h = 400$
  $h = 400 \div 38.48 = 10.4$ (1 d.p.)
- The height of the can is 10.4 cm.

THE CRASH COURSE

Surface area

The surface area of a 3D shape is the total area of all its surfaces.
The surface area of a cube is 6 × area of one face.
This cube has six faces each of area a^2, so its surface area is $6a^2$.

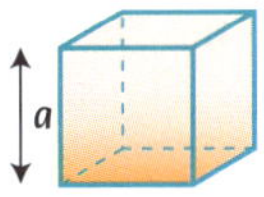

The surface area of a cuboid is
2 × area of top face + 2 × area of front face + 2 × area of side face.

The cuboid has six faces.
These are two top faces of area $(a \times b)$, two front faces of area $(b \times c)$ and two side faces of area $(c \times a)$, so its surface area is $(2 \times a \times b) + (2 \times b \times c) + (2 \times c \times a)$.

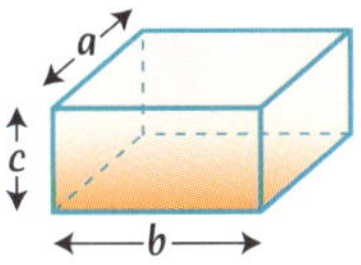

Capacity

The capacity of a container is the amount of space inside it. The capacity usually measures how much liquid or gas a container can hold.
Capacity is measured in units such as litres, centilitres and millilitres.
Capacity and volume are related, because 1000 cm^3 = 1 litre and 1 cm^3 = 1 millilitre.

EXAMPLE

One litre of water is poured into a cuboidal tank with base dimensions 10 cm by 40 cm.
What is the depth (d in cm) of water in the tank?

- The volume of water in the tank is 1 litre = 1000 cm^3 (work in the same units)
- The volume of water is $10 \times 40 \times d = 400 \times d$ cm^3
- $400 \times d = 1000$ and $d = 1000 \div 400 = 2.5$ cm

Dimensions

The units used to measure a quantity identify what type of quantity is being measured. For example if a quantity is measured in m^2 it is an area. Similarly, a quantity measured in cm is a length and a quantity measured in cm^3 is a volume.

Working with dimensions

What quantity does the formula $4\pi r^2$ represent if r is a length?
The dimensions are $[\text{length}]^2$ so this will be an area formula.

Tip:
4 and π are numbers which don't have units so they don't affect the dimensions.

Cancelling dimensions

Dimensions can be simplified in the same way as fractions.

What quantity does F measure if $F = \dfrac{d(a+b)}{c}$ and a, b, c and d are lengths?

The dimension are $\left[\dfrac{\text{length} \times (\text{length} + \text{length})}{\text{length}}\right] = \left[\dfrac{\text{length} \times (\text{length})}{\text{length}}\right] = [\text{length}]$

So F is a measure of length.

Tip:
The dimension of a [length + length] is a [length] dimension.

KEY FACTS AND SKILLS

- **the net of a solid** is a 2D shape which could be folded up to form the solid
- **the volume of a cube** is length × length × length
- **the volume of a cuboid** is length × width × width
- **the volume of a prism** is area of cross-section × length
- **the volume of a cylinder** is $\pi \times (\text{radius})^2 \times$ height
- **surface area** is the total area of all the surfaces of a solid
- **volume and capacity** are related, since 1 litre = 1000 cm^3
- **dimensions** can be used to identify formulae

EXAM PRACTICE QUESTIONS

1 The roof space in a house is to be converted into a play room. The loft is in the form of a triangular prism with the dimensions shown. To work out the heating requirements the volume of the room must be found. Calculate this volume. Give your answer to the nearest 10 m^3.

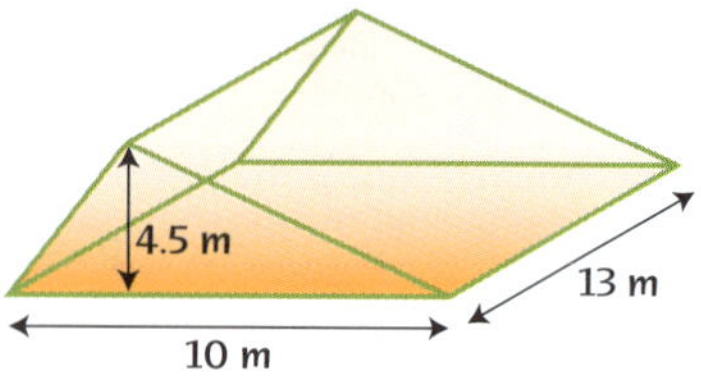

2 a) Find the volume of this cuboid.

b) Draw two possible nets for the cuboid.

c) Write down the dimensions of two more cuboids with the same volume.

d) The volume is increased by 25%. Write down possible dimensions for the new cuboid.

e) What is the surface area of the original cuboid?

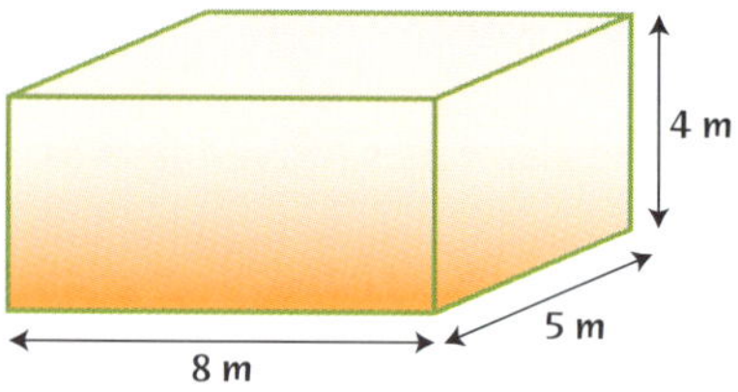

3 Draw a net of a tetrahedron.

4 A can has diameter 8 cm and height 11.5 cm.

a) What is the volume of the can? Give your answer to the nearest whole number of cm^3.

b) A box in the shape of a cuboid has base dimensions 48 cm by 32 cm. What is the maximum number of cans that could stand on this area?

c) If two layers of cans can be stacked in the box, what is the height of the box?

d) What is the volume of the box?

e) If the box is full of cans, what is the volume of the empty space?

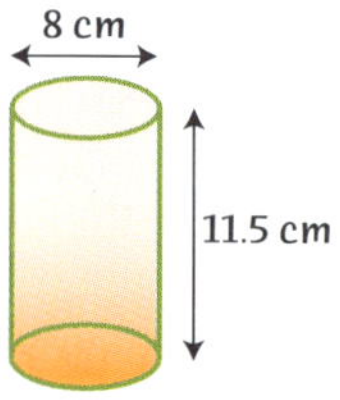

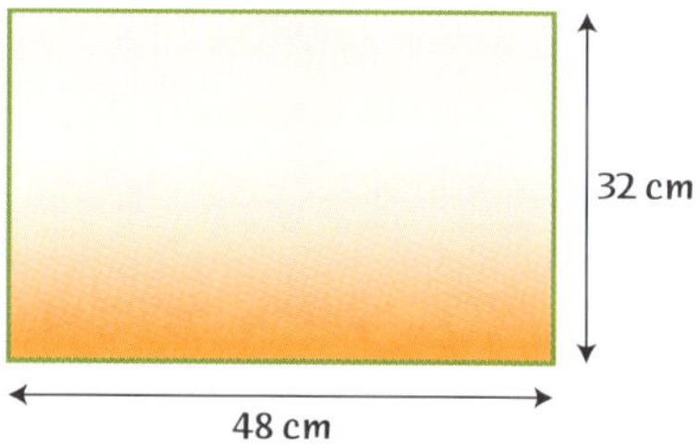

5 One of the formulae listed below is used to calculate the curved surface area of this tube. Identify the correct formula and give a reason for your answer.

$2\pi h(r + R)^2$

$2\pi h(R - r)^2$

$2\pi h(r + R)$

$2\pi h^2(r + R)^2$

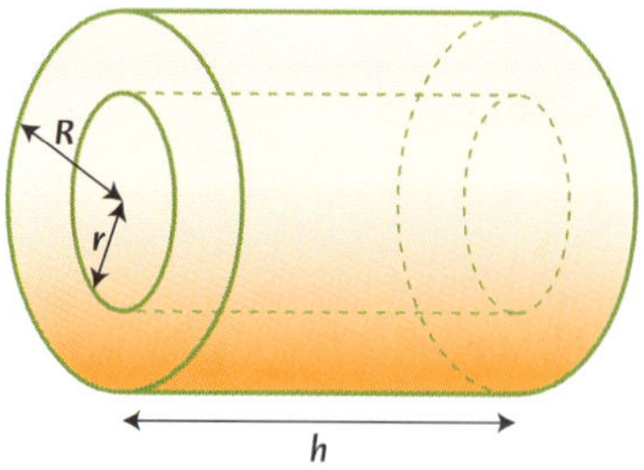

6 A cylindrical garden tub is filled with 75 litres of soil. The depth of the soil must be 40 cm. What is the diameter of the tub?

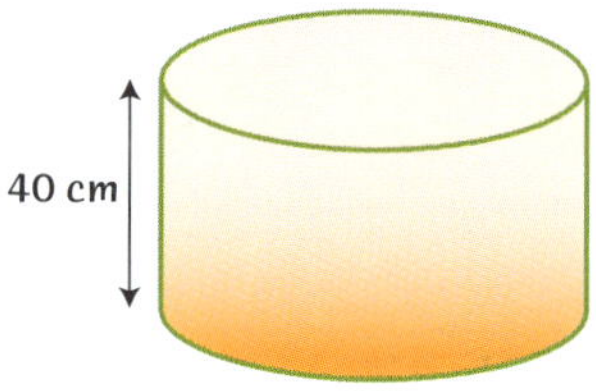

Revision Unit 19

Data

The Check Up

1 The pie chart shows the different types of transport 450 children use to go to school. Measure the angle for tram, then work out how many

children travel by tram. ______________

What is the percentage of children who walk? ______________

Types of transport used by 450 children

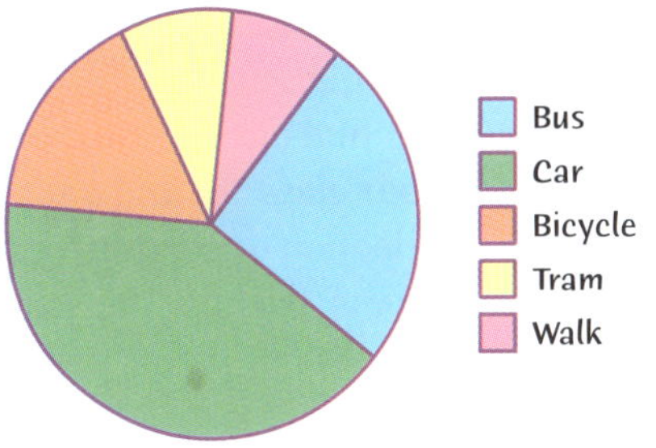

2 The table shows the numbers of people who go to a night class on Tuesdays. Draw a pie chart to show the subjects they study.

Class	Number
French	12
Bridge	8
Yoga	16
Art	4
Squash	20

3 The table shows how long 31 people have to wait to be seen in a clinic. Draw a histogram showing the waiting times of these patients.

Waiting time t in minutes	Number of patients
$0 \leq t < 20$	4
$20 \leq t < 40$	6
$40 \leq t < 60$	8
$60 \leq t < 80$	9
$80 \leq t < 100$	3
$100 \leq t < 120$	1

4 Draw a frequency polygon for the hospital waiting times in the table in question 3.

Mark yourself *(see answers on pages 106–107)*

- Just a few wrong? You're geared up for the Exam Practice Questions. Go for it!
- More than a few wrong? Boost your learning powers by taking the Crash Course before you tackle the Exam Practice Questions.

/ 5

THE CRASH COURSE

Collecting data

In statistics, information may be called **data**.
Data can be collected using **questionnaires**, **observation sheets** or **databases**.

Questionnaires

Questionnaires are lists of questions. They should be written so that they have short, clear answers, preferably 'yes' or 'no'. The questions must be fair or neutral without **bias**.
For example, to find out about the pocket money given to members of your class you should collect data from everyone in your class. To find out about the pocket money of all the children in your school you should collect data from a selection or **sample**, representative of the whole school. This means a selection of children from each class, not just your friends! The sample should be **random**.

Frequency tables

Once the data is collected, it must be sorted out. One way to do this is to use frequency tables.

Pocket money in £s	Tally	Frequency
0 to less than 1	𝍸 𝍸 III	13
1 to less than 2	𝍸 𝍸 𝍸 𝍸 I	21

and so on.

Tip:
Remember the data you collect is only as good as the representative sample you use.

Displaying data

Data can be displayed as:

- pictograms — a symbol represents a given quantity of information
- bar charts — each separate bar represents a specific piece of data
- line graphs — the intermediate values on the graph may or may not have any meaning
- pie charts — the data is shared amongst 360° and the angle for each piece of data is worked out. As 100% of the data is represented by 360°, 1% of the data is represented by $360° \div 100 = 3.6°$.

Steps for drawing pie charts

The table shows the amount of money (in £s) taken in a school tuck shop in a week.

Day	Monday	Tuesday	Wednesday	Thursday	Friday
Money	1.40	4.20	12.20	15.10	7.10

Use a pie chart to show the data.

1 Find the total amount. Total money in £s is:
$1.40 + 4.20 + 12.20 + 15.10 + 7.10 = 40.00$

2 Find the fraction of the total amount for each item of data.
Then multiply this fraction by 360° to work out the angles.
For Monday the fraction is $\frac{1.40}{40.00}$ so the angle is $\frac{1.40}{40.00} \times 360° = 12.6°$

3 Now draw the pie chart, starting with the smallest angle.

Money taken in a school tuck shop

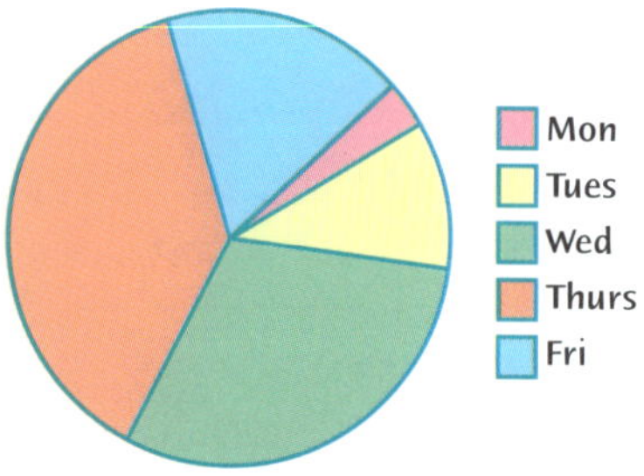

How to use pie charts

You must be able to read information from a given pie chart.
A pie chart showing the fruit eaten in a class during one week has an angle of 63° for peaches. If a total of 240 fruits were eaten, find the number of peaches.
The fraction for peaches is $\frac{63}{360}$. The number of peaches is $\frac{63}{360} \times 240 = 42$.

The Crash Course

Equal width histograms

Histograms look like bar charts. The difference is that each bar in a histogram represents a range of values. The data is grouped in intervals or **classes** of equal size or width.

Steps for making a histogram

Plot a histogram of the data in the following table giving the exam marks for 90 students.

Exam mark	0–10	11–20	21–30	31–40	41–50	51–60	61–70	71–80	81–90	91–100
Number of students (frequency)	3	6	12	13	18	17	12	5	3	1

1. Draw the axes. The vertical axis is the number of students (frequency).
2. Mark the class boundaries on the horizontal axis.
3. Mark the number of students for each class, and now just draw the bars.

Exam marks for 90 students

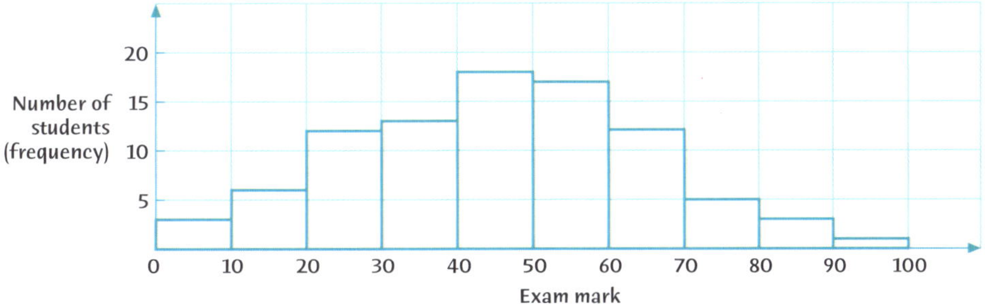

Frequency polygons

These are based on histograms. If the histogram is already drawn plot a point in the **middle** of the top of each bar and join these points to make a polygon. The result is the same as plotting the middle of the class interval on the horizontal axis against the frequency on the vertical axis.

The frequency polygon of the data given in the table above looks like this.

The broken line is the polygon.

A polygon is a closed shape, so extend the lines at the start and finish to meet the horizontal axis.

Exam marks for 90 students

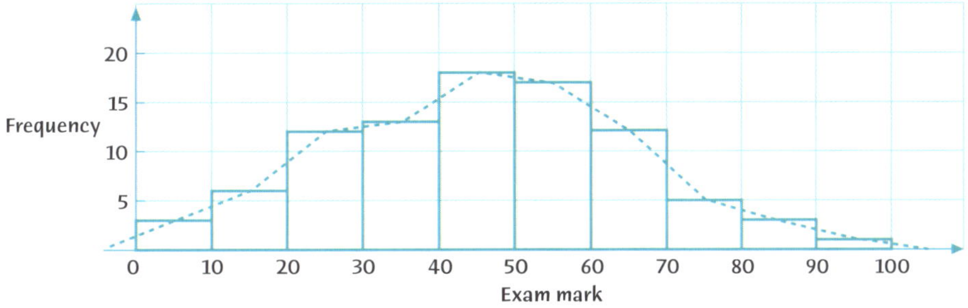

Key facts and skills

- collect data using a representative random sample without bias
- use tallies to make frequency tables
- display data using:
  - pictograms
  - bar charts
  - pie charts
  - line graphs
- plot equal width histograms by marking the class boundaries on the horizontal axis
- plot frequency polygons using the middle of each class interval

EXAM PRACTICE QUESTIONS

1 The table gives a breakdown of crimes recorded by the police one year.

Crime	% of total
Burglary	22
Theft	52
Criminal damage	16
Fraud and forgery	4
Violence against person	6

Show this information on a pie chart.

2 Matt wants to find out about the weights of the pupils in his year group. Make a table to show how he could record the information.

3 The pie chart shows the costs of running a small factory for one month. The total cost of running the factory is £10 800.

a) How much was spent on salaries?

b) How much was spent on production?

c) £1200 was spent on finance. Calculate angle x.

d) Calculate angle y.

Running costs of a factory

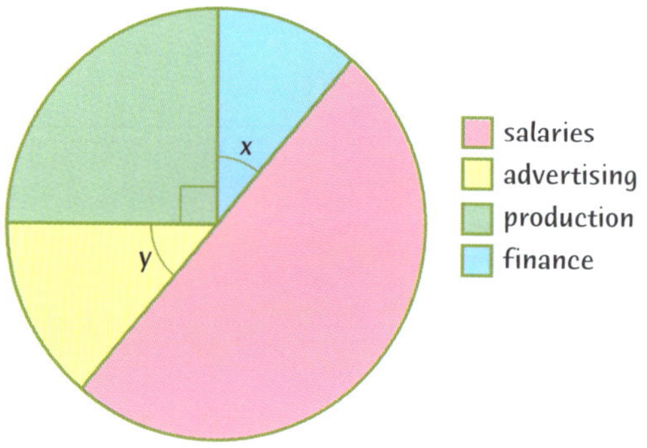

4 A farmer grew two varieties of potatoes. The table gives information about the weight of 100 plants of each variety.

Weight of potatoes for each w kg	Number of plants of Big spud	Number of plants of Smashing spud
$0 \leqslant w < 0.5$	0	0
$0.5 \leqslant w < 1.0$	2	1
$1.0 \leqslant w < 1.5$	10	5
$1.5 \leqslant w < 2.0$	59	36
$2.0 \leqslant w < 2.5$	21	33
$2.5 \leqslant w < 3.0$	8	25
$3.0 \leqslant w < 3.5$	0	0

a) Draw a frequency polygon for each variety of potato.

b) Which variety of potato gives the heavier crop?

c) Which type of potato has more variation in the weight of its crop? Give a reason for your answer.

Revision Unit 20

Averages and ranges

The Check Up

1 The table shows the marks out of 10 scored by 55 pupils in a test.

Mark	0	1	2	3	4	5	6	7	8	9	10
Frequency	1	1	3	5	6	12	13	8	4	2	0

Find:

a) the modal mark ______

b) the median mark ______

c) the mean mark ______

d) the range of marks. ______

2 The table shows the ages, in years, of all the 86 people living in one street.

Age y	$0 \leq y < 20$	$20 \leq y < 40$	$40 \leq y < 60$	$60 \leq y < 80$	$80 \leq y < 100$
Number of people	21	24	30	9	2

a) Write down the modal class. ______

b) In which class does the median lie? ______

c) Work out the estimated mean age in years. ______

3 The cumulative frequency curve shows the times 80 children take to get to school.

a) From the graph, find the median time. ______

b) From the graph, find the upper and lower quartiles. ______ ______

c) Work out the interquartile range. ______

d) How many children take more than 45 minutes to get to school? ______

Times taken by 80 children to get to school

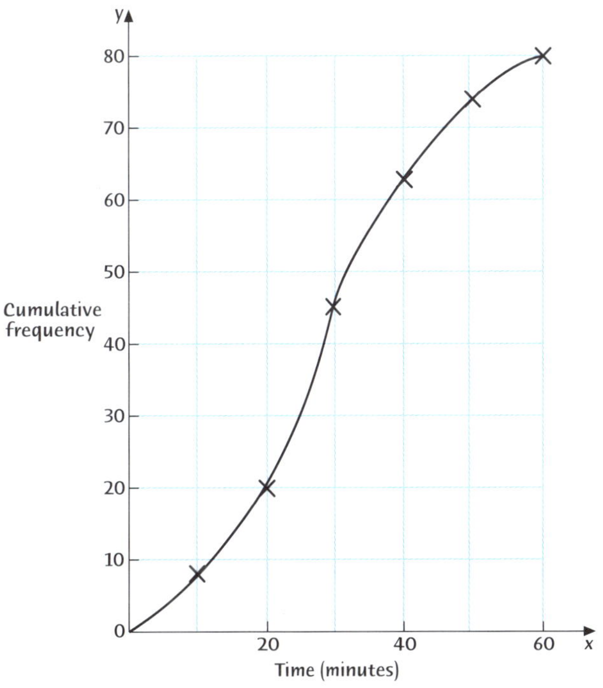

Mark yourself (see answers on page 107)

- Just a few wrong? You're geared up for the Exam Practice Questions. Go for it!
- More than a few wrong? Boost your learning powers by taking the Crash Course before you tackle the Exam Practice Questions.

/ 12

THE CRASH COURSE

Range

The is the difference between the highest and lowest values in a set of data.

Averages

Statisticians use three **averages**. These are the **mean**, the **mode** and the **median**.

Mean or arithmetic average

This is the sum of all the values divided by the number of values. It takes account of all the values and may be described as a 'typical value' for a range of data.

The formula to find the mean is $\frac{\text{total of values}}{\text{number of values}}$.

Tip: Mean is the most commonly-used average.

Mode

This is the value which occurs most frequently. For example, a shoe-shop manager would use the mode to see which sizes are most popular.

Tip: Mode means most.

Median

This is the middle value when all the values are arranged in order of size. For example, it is useful when the end values are very different from the rest of the values.

If there are n values and n is odd, the median is the $\frac{1}{2}(n+1)$th value.

If there are n values and n is even, the median is half-way between the two middle numbers.

Tip: Median is middle.

EXAMPLE

This list shows the numbers of goals scored in 11 matches by a school in a term.

2, 4, 5, 0, 4, 3, 2, 2, 3, 5, 1

Find the mode, median and mean score. Write down the range.

- The most frequent number is 2 so the mode is 2.
- To find the median, arrange the data in order of size.
  0, 1, 2, 2, 2, [3,] 3, 4, 4, 5, 5
  There are 11 items of data so the middle item is the sixth.
  The median is 3.
- The total number of goals is $2+4+5+0+4+3+2+2+3+5+1=31$
  The total number of games is 11.
  The mean number of goals is $31 \div 11 = 2.82$ (2 d.p.)
- The range is the difference between the highest and lowest values, $5-0=5$

Frequency tables and the mean

The formula for finding the mean is $= \frac{\Sigma(f \times x)}{\Sigma f}$. Σ is a Greek letter and stands for 'the sum of', x is the data value and f is the frequency.

Steps for finding the mean

The table shows the numbers of goals (x) scored for a series of matches.

Find the mean number of goals.

Goals(x)	1	2	3	4	5	6	
Frequency (f)	15	19	18	16	21	11	$\Sigma f = 100$
$f \times x$	$15 \times 1 = 15$	$19 \times 2 = 38$	$18 \times 3 = 54$	$16 \times 4 = 64$	$21 \times 5 = 105$	$11 \times 6 = 66$	$\Sigma(f \times x) = 342$

1. Add another row and work out $f \times x$.
2. Total the frequency row to find Σf.
3. Total the $f \times x$ row to find $\Sigma(f \times x)$.
4. Put the numbers into the formula: Mean number of goals is $\frac{\Sigma(f \times x)}{\Sigma f} = \frac{342}{100} = 3.4$

THE CRASH COURSE

Frequency tables, mode and median

- The mode is the item of data with the highest frequency.
  In the previous example the highest frequency is 21 (for 5 goals) so the mode is 5.
- The median is the middle value. Again in the previous example, the median is the 50th goal, so the median is 3 since $15 + 19 + 16 = 50$.

Frequency tables, grouped data and estimated mean

In **grouped data**, the values are given in ranges, rather than as exact numbers. It is not possible to know where in the group each item of data lies, so assume all the data in any given group lies in the middle of that group. Then work out (frequency × the midpoint value) for each group.

The formula for the estimated mean is $\frac{\Sigma(f \times \text{midpoint value})}{\Sigma f}$.

Steps for finding an estimated mean

Find the estimated mean of the heights (h) of 80 children in a school, using the data in the table below.

Height h in cm	Frequency (f)	Midpoint value (x)	$f \times$ midpoint value ($f \times x$)
$80 \leqslant h < 90$	4	85	$4 \times 85 = 340$
$90 \leqslant h < 100$	11	95	$11 \times 95 = 1045$
$100 \leqslant h < 110$	19	105	$19 \times 105 = 1995$
$110 \leqslant h < 120$	27	115	$27 \times 115 = 3105$
$120 \leqslant h < 130$	19	125	$19 \times 125 = 2375$
	$\Sigma f = 80$		$\Sigma(f \times \text{midpoint value}) = 8860$

1. Work out the midpoint value of the data and add another column.
2. Add yet another column and work out the frequency × the midpoint value.
3. Total the frequency column to find $\Sigma f = 80$.
4. Total the last column to find $\Sigma(f \times \text{midpoint value}) = 8860$.
5. Put the numbers into the formula.

   Estimated mean height in cm is $\frac{\Sigma(f \times \text{midpoint value})}{\Sigma f} = \frac{8860}{80} = 110.8$ (1 d.p.)

Frequency tables, modal class and grouped data

The mode cannot be found, but the **modal class** is the group with the highest frequency. In the data above the modal class is the one with the highest frequency, which is 110–120.

KEY FACTS AND SKILLS

- **mode** means most, **median** is middle
- **mean** is $\frac{\text{total of values}}{\text{number of values}}$
- **range** is highest value − lowest value
- using a **frequency table**: the mean is $\frac{\Sigma(f \times x)}{\Sigma f}$
- using a **grouped frequency table**, the **estimated mean** is $\frac{\Sigma(f \times \text{midpoint value})}{\Sigma f}$

THE CRASH COURSE

Cumulative frequency graphs

A cumulative frequency graph can be plotted and then used to find the median.

Steps for plotting cumulative frequency graphs

Plot a cumulative frequency graph for the following data which shows the heights (h) of a class of 50 children, measured to the nearest cm.

Height	$100 < h \leq 110$	$110 < h \leq 120$	$120 < h \leq 130$	$130 < h \leq 140$	$140 < h \leq 150$	$150 < h \leq 160$
Frequency	5	8	10	15	8	4
Cumulative frequency	5	$5 + 8 = 13$	$13 + 10 = 23$	$23 + 15 = 38$	$38 + 8 = 46$	$46 + 4 = 50$

1 Add another row to the table and work out the cumulative frequencies.
2 Now circle the upper boundaries of each class.
3 Plot the circled data on the horizontal axis and the cumulative frequency on the vertical axis.
4 Join the points in a smooth curve.

- The **median** is the middle value (total number ÷ 2). Draw a line from the halfway point on the vertical axis to the curve, then down to the **horizontal** axis and read off the value of the median, which is 131.5 cm.
- The **lower quartile** is the quarter-way value (total number ÷ 4). Draw a line from the quarter-way position to the curve, then down to the horizontal axis and read off the value of the lower quartile, which is 120 cm.
- Similarly the **upper quartile** is the three-quarter way value (total number ÷ 4 × 3). Draw a line from the three-quarter way position to the curve, then, from this point, down to the horizontal axis and read off the value of the upper quartile, which is 139.5 cm.

Heights of a class of 50 children

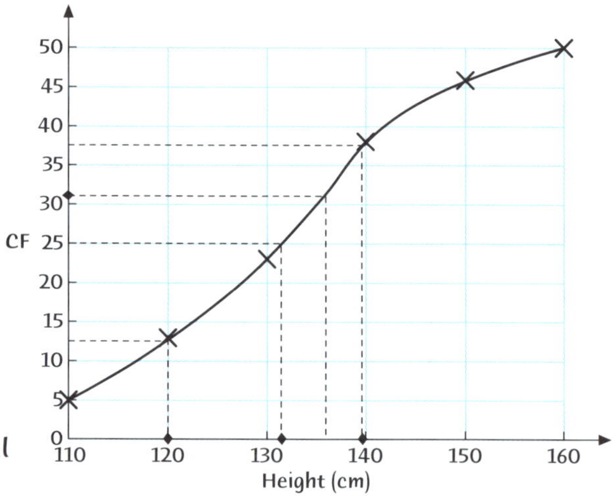

- The **interquartile range** is the difference between the upper and lower quartiles. $139.5 - 120 = 19.5$ cm

Tip: The interquartile range gives information about the spread of the middle half of the data.

How to use cumulative frequency graphs

A cumulative frequency graph can be used to find out how many results are more than or less than a given value. Refer to the graph drawn above. To find the number of children with heights less than 136 cm, find 136 on the horizontal axis and draw a line to the curve. Then draw a line from this point across to the vertical axis and read off the value.

31 children have heights less than or equal to 136 cm.

$50 - 31 = 19$ children have heights more than 136 cm.

KEY FACTS AND SKILLS

- to plot cumulative frequency graphs:
  plot cumulative frequency on the vertical axis
  plot the top value of the range of data on the horizontal axis
- the median is the halfway mark
- the lower quartile is the quarter-way mark, the upper quartile is the three-quarter way mark
- the interquartile range = upper quartile − lower quartile

EXAM PRACTICE QUESTIONS

1 The bar chart shows the shoe sizes for 60 female students.

a) Find the mean shoe size.

b) What is the median shoe size?

c) What is the modal shoe size?

d) What is the best average to use?

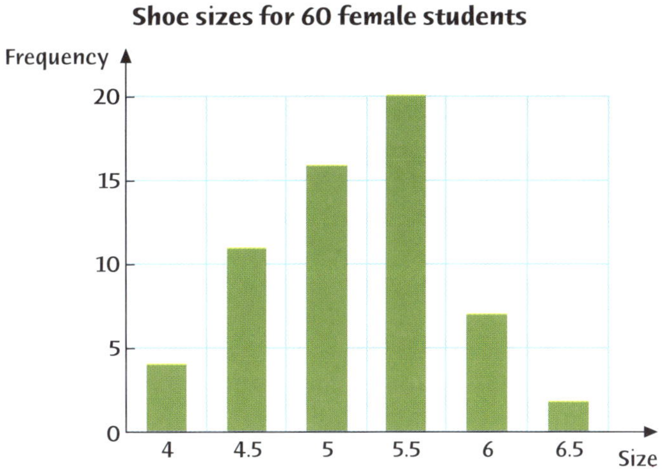

2 The times 100 children took to get to school are recorded in the table below.

Journey time t in minutes	Number of children f	Cumulative frequency
$0 \leq t < 10$	8	
$10 \leq t < 20$	14	
$20 \leq t < 30$	25	
$30 \leq t < 40$	35	
$40 \leq t < 60$	11	
$60 \leq t < 80$	5	
$80 \leq t < 120$	2	

a) Complete the cumulative frequency column and draw a cumulative frequency curve showing the journey times.

b) Use your graph to find the median.

c) Use your graph to find the upper and lower quartile.

d) What is the interquartile range? Comment on this result.

e) Use your graph to find the percentage of children who took more than 45 minutes to get to school.

3 Refer to the table from question 2. Work out an estimated mean. Explain why the mean is an estimation.

Revision Unit 21

Scatter diagrams

The Check Up

The table gives the marks out of 10 and the time spent on a piece of maths homework for nine pupils. Use it to answer the questions.

Pupil	A	B	C	D	E	F	G	H	I
Time in minutes	60	55	30	10	25	19	40	43	40
Mark	9	8	6	1	4	2	6	8	7

1 Plot this data on a scatter diagram. Draw the line of best fit and comment on the correlation between the two sets of data.

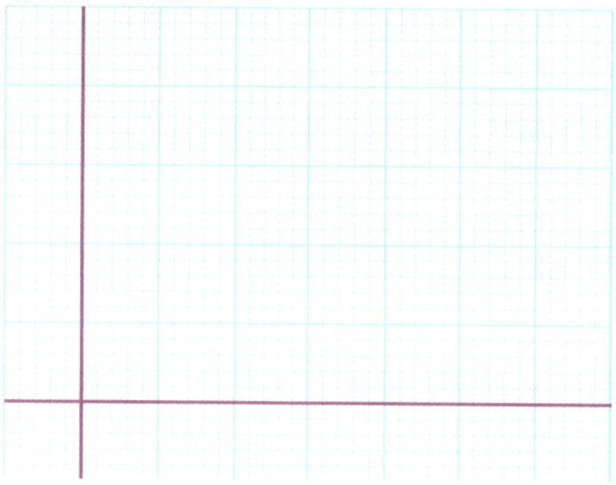

____

2 If a student got a mark of 5 on her homework what time might she have spent on her homework?

____

3 Explain why you cannot extend the graph to find the maths mark of a student who took 80 minutes on his homework.

____

____

Mark yourself *(see answers on page 108)*

- Just a few wrong? You're geared up for the Exam Practice Questions. Go for it!
- More than a few wrong? Boost your learning powers by taking the Crash Course before you tackle the Exam Practice Questions.

/ 5

The Crash Course

Scatter diagrams

A scatter diagram is a graph which shows if there is a relationship between two sets of data. If a linear relationship does exist, it is possible to draw the line of best fit. This is a line which is drawn so that there are roughly the same number of points above the line as there are below it.

No correlation

If the points plotted are randomly scattered, there is no correlation between the two sets of data.

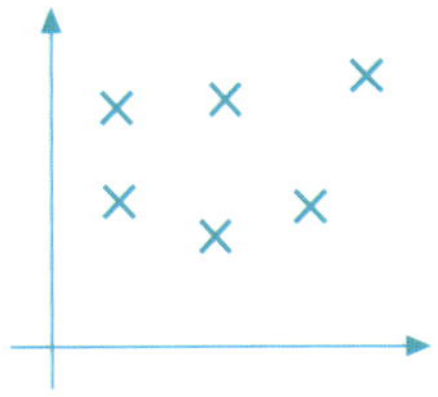

Strong correlation

If the points plotted are close to the line of best fit, there is strong correlation between the two sets of data.

If as one item of data increases so does the corresponding item, there is positive correlation between the two sets of data.

If as one item of data increases the corresponding item of data decreases, there is negative correlation between the two sets of data.

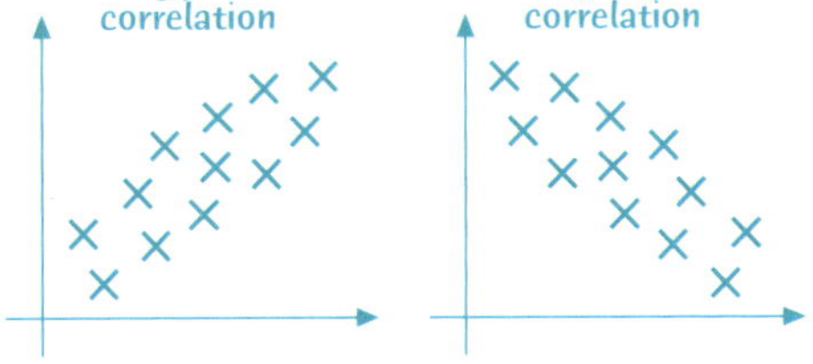

Weak correlation

If the points plotted form a pattern around the line of best fit, but are not close to it, there is weak correlation between the two sets of data.

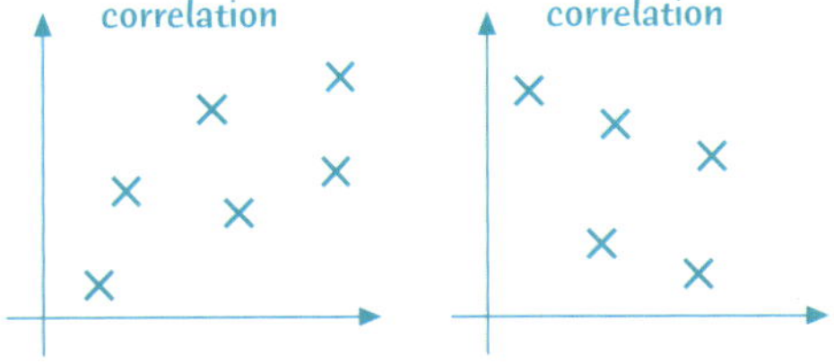

Example

The table gives the amount of time spent on Maths homework and the amount of time spent watching TV for six pupils.

Pupil	A	B	C	D	E	F
Maths time in minutes	60	55	30	10	40	40
TV time in minutes	15	25	80	120	60	55

Plot a scatter diagram of the data, draw the line of best fit and comment on the results. If a pupil spent 90 minutes watching TV how long might they spend on their maths homework?

It doesn't really matter which way round the points are plotted, so plot the maths time on the horizontal axis and the TV time on the vertical axis.

There is strong negative correlation between the two sets of data.

Not surprisingly, the graph shows that more time spent watching TV is associated with less time spent on maths homework!

Draw a line at 90 minutes TV time to meet the line of best fit and then a line down to the horizontal axis. This shows the corresponding Maths time, which is 25 minutes.

Time spent on Maths homework and watching TV

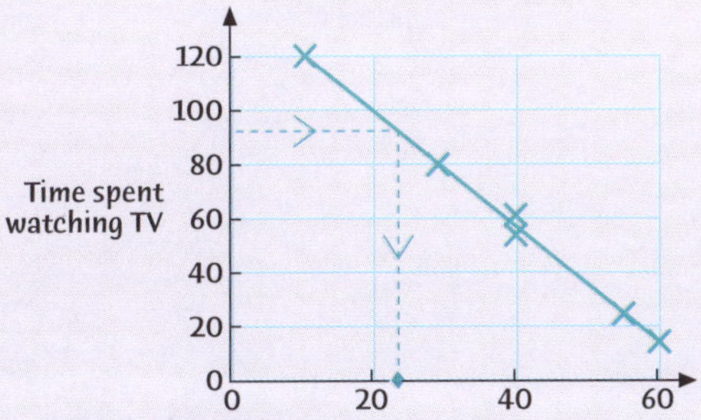

Key facts and skills

- a **scatter diagram** and the **line of best fit** shows relationships between sets of data
- **positive correlation** is shown by a positive gradient on the line of best fit
- **negative correlation** is shown by a negative gradient of the line of best fit
- correlation may be **strong**, **fairly strong** or **weak** and **positive** or **negative**
- a scatter diagram showing correlation can be used to **find the value of one item of data from another item of data**

EXAM PRACTICE QUESTIONS

1 Describe the correlation, if there is any, in these two diagrams.

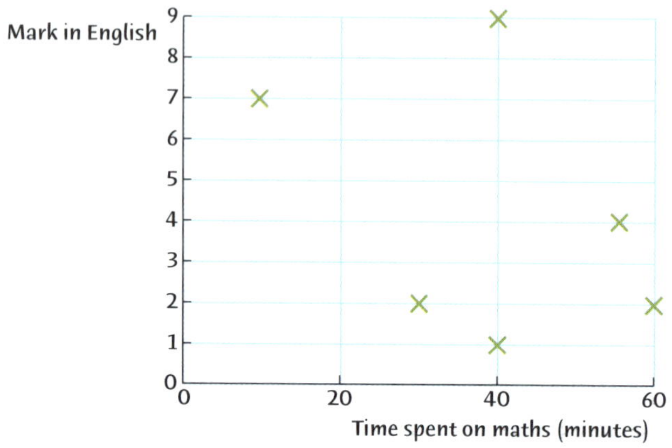

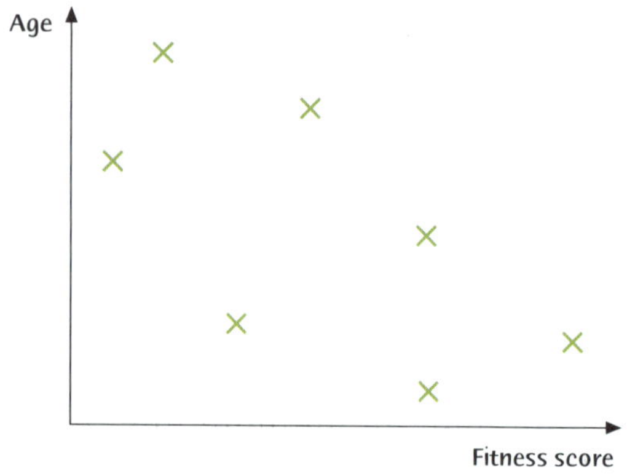

2 The following table shows the amount of rain, in cm, which fell at two weather stations, N and S, over one year.

	Jan	Feb	Mar	April	May	June	July	Aug	Sept	Oct	Nov	Dec
Station N	5.2	4.8	6.1	5.1	3.2	2.9	1.8	7.3		2.5	2.5	5.4
Station S	4.6	4.2	5.4	4.4	2.9	2.8	1.3	7.0	5.0	2.1	1.9	4.9

a) Work out the mean rainfall at Station S.

b) Plot the data on a scatter diagram.

c) Draw the line of best fit.

d) Comment on the correlation.

e) Station N failed to take a reading in September.
Using your diagram and the data from station S, what rainfall might Station N get in this month?

Revision Unit 22
Probability

The Check Up

1 The probability that it will rain on the day of the school fete is 0.35.

What is the probability that it will not rain? ____________

2 A biased spinner can land on 1, 2, 3 or 4. The probability of scoring a 1 is 0.3, the probability of scoring a 2 is 0.1 and the probability of scoring a 3 is 0.45.

What is the probability of scoring a 4? ____________

3 In a box of 20 sweets, nine are toffees, five are mints and six are fruit drops.
If a sweet is picked at random find the probability that:

a) is a toffee ____________

b) it is a mint or a toffee ____________

c) it is not a mint. ____________

4 In a biased die the probability of throwing a 6 is 0.08. If the die is thrown 100 times how many

6s would you expect to score? ____________

5 The probability that Rohit wins his tennis match is 0.55.
The probability that Fergus wins his tennis match is 0.75.

What is the probability that Rohit and Fergus both win their matches? ____________

6 A box contains twelve balls. Seven are new and five have been used.
A ball is selected at random and then replaced. A second ball is then selected. Show the outcomes on a tree diagram.

a) What is the probability of selecting a new ball first and then a used ball? ____________

b) What is the probability of selecting a new and a used ball in any order? ____________

c) Work out the probability of selecting at least one new ball. ____________

Mark yourself *(see answers on page 109)*

- Just a few wrong? You're geared up for the Exam Practice Questions. Go for it!
- More than a few wrong? Boost your learning powers by taking the Crash Course before you tackle the Exam Practice Questions.

/ 12

THE CRASH COURSE

Probability

In statistics, something that 'happens' is an **event** or **trial**. For example, throwing a die is an event. The result of an event is an **outcome** or a **result**. For example, when throwing a die there are six possible outcomes or scores. In a fair die, all outcomes are equally possible.

Probability is a measure of the likelihood of a particular outcome happening.

A **certainty** is something that is bound to happen, such as the sun coming up tomorrow.

An **impossibility** is something that cannot happen, such as a cow giving birth to a hen.

The probability of a certainty is 1 and the probability of an impossibility is 0.

An even chance or 50/50 chance has a probability of $\frac{1}{2}$ or 0.5 or 50%.

A probability must be a number from 0 to 1, so a probability which is negative or more than 1 is a wrong answer!

Tip: The more likely the result the nearer the probability is to 1.

A probability can be written as a fraction or as a decimal or as a percentage.

How to work out probabilities

Probabilities can be estimated by carrying out experiments or filling in data sheets. These are used to find how often different outcomes or results happen in a given number of events or trials. The relative frequency of a particular result is $\frac{\text{number of times the particular result occurs}}{\text{number of trials}}$. It is an estimate of the probability of the result.

If all the outcomes are equally likely, use a formula: $\text{P(outcome)} = \frac{\text{number of ways the outcome can occur}}{\text{number of possible outcomes}}$.

If you have fair a pack of cards and select a card at random, the probability of a red ace is $\frac{\text{number of red aces in the pack}}{\text{number of cards in the pack}}$.

$\text{P(red ace)} = \frac{2}{52} = \frac{1}{26}$

The 1 rules

- An outcome can either happen or not happen, so P(outcome not happening) = 1 − P(outcome happening)
- Provided that two or more results can't happen at the same time, the sum of all the probabilities of possible outcomes for an event is 1 .

EXAMPLES

- If the probability of getting to school on time is 0.8, then the probability of not getting to school on time is $1 - 0.8 = 0.2$.
- A football team can win, draw or lose. The probability of winning is 0.2 and the probability of losing is 0.5. What is the probability of drawing?
  Probability of drawing is $1 - (0.2 + 0.5) = 0.3$.

KEY FACTS AND SKILLS

- the **probability of a result** is a number from 0 to 1
- **relative frequency** is an experimental approximation to probability
- for **equally likely outcomes**, P(outcome) $= \frac{\text{number of ways the outcome can occur}}{\text{number of possible outcomes}}$
- **probability of a result not happening** = 1 − probability of the result happening.
- in a given situation the **sum of all possible probabilities** is 1 (provided the results can't happen at the same time)

THE CRASH COURSE

The expected number of times of getting a result

If the probability of getting a result is p and the experiment is done n times, then the expected number of times of getting a result is $n \times p$.

EXAMPLE

The probability of a rainy day in November is 0.3. There are 30 days in November.
So the expected number of rainy days is $30 \times 0.3 = 9$

The 'add' and the 'multiply' rules

The add rule (for mutually exclusive results)

- If two results cannot happen at the same time, they are **mutually exclusive**.
  $P(A \text{ or } B) = P(A) + P(B)$

EXAMPLE

In a bag of mixed sweets the probability of picking a peppermint is 0.3 and the probability of picking a fruit drop is 0.4.
What is the probability of picking a peppermint or fruit drop in any one go?
A peppermint and fruit drop can't both be picked at the same time.
The probability of picking a peppermint or fruit drop in any one go $= P(P) + P(F) = 0.3 + 0.4 = 0.7$.

The multiply rule (for results which are independent)

- If the outcome of one event does not affect the outcome of another event, they are **independent**.
  $P(A \text{ and } B) = P(A) \times P(B)$

EXAMPLE

A coin is tossed and a die is rolled. What is the probability of getting a tail and a six?
Getting a tail does not depend on getting a six so the probability of getting a tail and a six $= P(T) \times P(\text{six}) = \frac{1}{2} \times \frac{1}{6} = \frac{1}{12}$.

Using both the add and multiply rules

A bag contains four red balls and six white balls. One ball is taken out of the bag at random and then replaced. Then a second ball is taken out at random. What is the probability that the balls selected are different colours?

$P(R) = \frac{4}{10} = 0.4$

$P(W) = \frac{6}{10} = 0.6$

To work out the probability of both balls being different colours:

- work out the probability that the first ball is red **and** the second is white
  $P(R \text{ and } W) = P(R) \times P(W) = 0.4 \times 0.6 = 0.24$
- then work out the probability that the first ball is white **and** the second is red
  $P(W \text{ and } R) = P(W) \times P(R) = 0.6 \times 0.4 = 0.24$
- add the two probabilities found.
  $P(R \text{ and } W) \text{ or } P(W \text{ and } R) = P(R \text{ and } W) + P(W \text{ and } R) = 0.24 + 0.24 = 0.48$

KEY FACTS AND SKILLS

- **expected number of times** of getting a result is $n \times p$
- for two **mutually exclusive events**, if you can reword the question using **OR**, **add** (+)
- for two **independent events**, if you can reword the question using **AND**, **multiply** (×)

THE CRASH COURSE

Tree diagrams

More complicated problems involving probabilities can be displayed and worked out using tree diagrams.
On the way to school Kate goes through two sets of traffic lights. The probability of her being stopped at the first set of lights is 0.2 and at the second set of lights it is 0.3.
On a tree diagram the results (or outcomes) look like this.

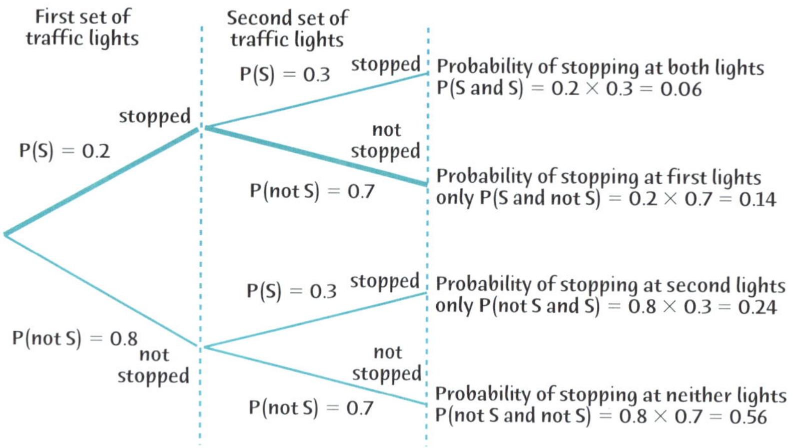

- To work out the probability of stopping at the first lights and not stopping at the second lights, follow along the paths in heavy lines and **multiply** the probabilities.
- To work out the probability of stopping at one set of lights only, work out the probability of stopping at the first lights and not stopping at the second, or not stopping at the first lights and stopping at the second.
  This is P(S and not S) or P(not S and S) so **add** the two probabilities.
  The probability of stopping at one set of lights only is
  P((S and not S) or (not S and S)) = 0.14 + 0.24 = 0.38

The 'at least' question

Look again at the example above.
The probability of stopping for at least one set of lights means the probability of stopping at the first or the second or both. Although it is possible to work out the separate probabilities and then add them, it's much quicker to use a '1' rule and work out the probability of stopping at *neither* set of lights which is $0.8 \times 0.7 = 0.56$.
Then the probability of stopping at *at least* one set of lights is $1 - 0.56 = 0.44$.

Tip: As a useful check, the sum of all the probabilities at the ends of the second branches must be 1.

In this example the probabilities at the ends of the branches are 0.06, 0.14, 0.24 and 0.56.
Then adding, $0.06 + 0.14 + 0.24 + 0.56 = 1$.

KEY FACTS AND SKILLS

- use **tree diagrams** to work out probabilities
- follow along two branches and **multiply the two probabilities**
- at the end of the branches **add the probabilities**

Exam Practice Questions

1 The probability that the 8 a.m. train is on time is 0.55.

a) What is the probability that the train is not on time?

b) If Sid used this train to travel to work for 12 weeks (he doesn't work at weekends) how many times would he expect the train not to be on time?

2 In a school the probability that a child chosen at random will pass a maths test is 0.8, and the probability that the child will pass a science test is 0.6.

a) Complete this tree diagram.

b) What is the probability that a child will pass both tests?

c) Work out the probability that a child will pass just one of these tests.

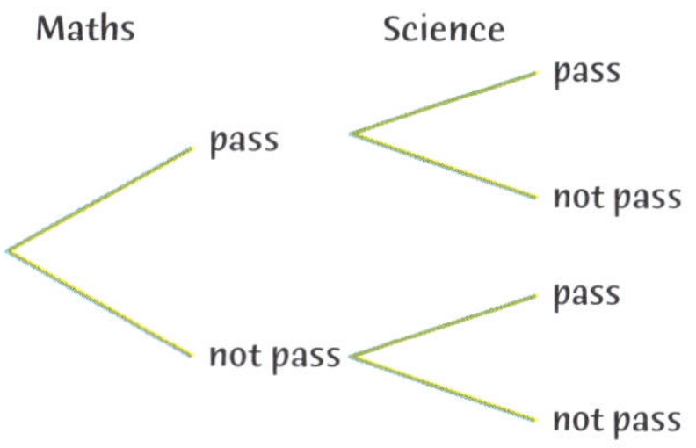

3

start		pit			★

A game is played with a fair four-sided die. If you land in the pit you go back to the start. You gain an extra turn if you land on the star.

a) What is the probability that you go back to the start on your first throw?

b) What is the probability that you gain a throw on your second turn?

4 A bag contains square, triangular and circular discs numbered 1, 2, 3 or 4. The table shows the probability of the different results when a disc is selected at random.

	Number on counter			
Shape of disc	1	2	3	4
□	0.1	0.2	0	0.1
△	0	0.1	0.2	0
○	0.1	0	0	0.2

a) What is the probability that it is ○ and numbered 4?

b) What is the probability that it is □ or numbered 3?

c) What is the probability that it is △ or numbered 2?

d) If there are 16 discs numbered 1, how many discs are there altogether?

5 There are two lucky dips at a fair. One has ten discs with four winning numbers. The other has eight discs with three winning numbers. Zeena takes a disc from both lucky dips.
By drawing a tree diagram or otherwise find the probability:

a) that she will pick two winning discs

b) that she will pick just one winning disc from either bag

c) that she will pick at least one winning disc.

ANSWERS

1 Number

The Check Up

1 a) 200 b) 156 c) 236.7 d) 166.67
e) 2.89 f) 22 000 g) 0.0002

2 a) 2, 3, 5, 7, 11, 13
b) 3, 6, 10, 15
c) 3, 6, 9, 12, 15
d) 3, 5, 15

3 $2 \times 3^3 \times 5 \times 7$

4 65.809 176 23, 65.8, 60

5 13.255 cm, 13.265 cm

6 2649, 2550

Exam Practice

1 a) 5, 4
Product means multiply, so look first at factors of 20.
b) 8
$8 \times 7 = 56$, $8 \times 3 = 24$
c) 23, 29, 31, 37
Look for numbers with just two factors.

2 a) $9.81\ \text{m/s}^2$
Look at the digit in the third decimal place. It is 7 so round up.
b) $9.8\ \text{m/s}^2$
Look at the third significant figure. It is 0 so round down.

3 a) 1.3425 m, 1.1525 m
To the nearest tenth of a centimetre means accuracy to 3 d.p. so add 0.0005.
b) 1.3415 m, 1.1515 m
Subtract 0.0005.

4 £40
The number of litres is approximately $600 \div 9$, the cost is approximately \$70 $\times$ 0.9, which is approximately £60 $\times$ 0.7.

5 3 minutes 21.455 seconds
The time is given correct to the second decimal place so subtract 0.005.

2 Powers and indices

The Check Up

1 a) 4060 b) 0.162 c) 0.00168 d) 2.73

2 a) 2^6 b) 1 c) $\frac{5}{36}$ d) 3 e) 5

3 a) 2.279×10^8 km b) 4.2×10^{-9} g

4 a) 1.33×10^{13} kg b) 2.8×10^{-4}, 1.5×10^1

5 a) 3.5 cm b) 2.52 cm

Exam Practice

1 a) 5.29×10^{-6}
Use the x^2 key: 0.000 005 29
b) 1.28×10^1
Use the x^y key (or y^x): 12.81…
c) 5.57×10^{-1}
Use the x^y key (or y^x) with +/– 0.557
d) 2.74 ($\times 10^0$)
Use the $\sqrt[3]{}$ key.

2 a) 3^7
Add the indices.
b) 16 or 4^2
Add -1 and 3.
c) 2^2 or 4
Subtract the indices.
d) 2^9
Multiply the indices.
e) 9 or 3^2
Write 9^2 as $(3^2)^2 = 3^4$, then subtract the indices.

3 $x = 4$, $y = 17$
Divide by 2 four times, then divide by 3.

4 a) 2.998×10^8 m/s
The decimal point 'moves' $\leftarrow$ 8 places.
b) 6.7×10^{-11}
The decimal point 'moves' $\rightarrow$ 11 places.

5 0.726 160 249, 0.726
Use your memory or brackets for denominator.

6 2.867×10^{-2}
Use your **EXP** *or* **EE** *button.*

7 1.52×10^{12}
Density is mass $\div$ volume, so density $= \dfrac{1.99 \times 10^{30}}{1.31 \times 10^{18}}$ kg/km³

3 Percentages

The Check Up

1 $41\frac{2}{3}\%$ or 41.67%, 74%
2 21
3 £256.50
4 £24.68
5 £612.50
6 £4375
7 30
8 £15, £3
9 $\frac{12}{20} = \frac{2}{5}$
10 87.4%
11 30%

Exam Practice

1

5%	0.05	$\frac{5}{100} = \frac{1}{20}$
37.5%	0.375	$\frac{3}{8}$
55%	0.55	$\frac{55}{100} = \frac{11}{20}$

2 a) £45.10
Find 18% of 55, it is a reduction so subtract this from the price.
b) £52.88
Find 17.5% of 45 then add this to the price.
c) £50.67
Find $\frac{2}{3}$ of £76.

3 20%
Find $\dfrac{\text{actual decrease}}{15.60} \times 100\%$.

4 400
To find the original number divide by the percentage.

5 £64.29
He sells at a loss, so £45 is 70% of the original price. To find the original price divide by the percentage.
6 a) £48 150
Add 7% of £45 000 to the original price.
b) £55 126.94
Use the multiplying factor 1.07^3 on the original price.
c) £174 136 to nearest £
Use the multiplying factor 1.07^{20} on the original price.
7 a) £648.15, £226.85 = £227 to the nearest £.
£875 is 135% of original price, so the original (cost) price is £648.15 and the profit is the difference between selling price and cost price.
b) 46.3%
Work out $\frac{\text{profit}}{648.15} \times 100\%$.

4 Ratio, conversions and compound measure

The Check Up

1 a) 1 : 1.4
b) Fin £375, Rob £225, Mark £150
c) 1 : 200 000
d) 1.5 km
2 a) 188 miles (or 180 miles, or 190 miles)
b) 82p
c) 3.5 pints
3 a) 100 g
b) 72.20 euros
c) £35.29
d) 1375 g
e) 357 books
4 72 km/h

Exam Practice

1 a) 25
Divide by 12 to get one part, multiply by 5 to get the number of fruit drops.
b) 45
Divide by 4 to get 1 part, multiply by 9 to get the total.
c) 10
The ratio is 2 : 1 so the number of toffees is 30.
2 Big value
Find the cost of 50 ml in each bottle: 'Big value' 14.9p, 'Best value' 15p, 'Good value' 15.6p, so 'Big value' is the best buy.
3 a) 1 : 50
Work in the same units, the ratio is 2 : 100.
b) 275 cm
Multiply by the map scale.
c) 1.5 cm
Divide by the plan scale.
4 a) 472 francs
Work it out as 50 × 9.64 − 10.
b) £1.87
Work it out as 18 ÷ 9.64.
c) 85p
2.2 pounds ≈ 1 kg so divide by 2.2.
5 48.6 mph
The total distance is 170 miles, total time is 3.5 hours.
6 a) 13.5 inches (or 0.35 m)
Work in inches, 1 m ≈ 39 inches.
b) 83p
Find the cost of fabric per inch, then multiply by 13.5.

5 Algebra

The Check Up

1 a) $-3a + 4ab - b$
b) $2x^2 + 5xy - 4y^2$
c) a^6
d) $15p^6$
e) $5x^2$
f) $64x^9$
2 a) $8y^2 + 12y$
b) $-4x^2 + 2x$
c) $x^2 + 7x + 10$
d) $6b^2 - 7b - 3$
e) $9a^2 + 30a + 25$
3 a) $5a^2 - 2a$
b) $-x^2 + 15x$ or $15x - x^2$
c) $5 - 2x$
4 20.39 m/s (giving the answer to the same degree of accuracy as the question)
5 46.4 °F, 29.4 °C

Exam Practice

1 $7x - xy + 7y$
Remember that xy and yx are like terms.
2 $3x^2 + 13x - 10$
Use FOIL, then collect like x-terms
3 $A^2 - a^2$
A and a are not like terms, but Aa and aA are, the −Aa and + aA terms 'cancel out'.
4 $3y + 4$
Remember to add all three sides.
5 a) $z^2 + 3z$
Write $z \times (z + 3)$ *as* $z(z + 3)$.
b) $z^2 + z - 2$
Write $(z - 1) \times (z + 2)$ *as* $(z - 1)(z + 2)$, *use FOIL and collect like z−terms.*
6 Work out $(a + 1)^2$
$(a + 1)^2$ *is* $(a + 1)(a + 1)$ *so use FOIL.*
Work out $-2(a - 1)$ *and collect like terms.*
Remember $(-) \times (-) = (+)$ *so* $-2 \times -1 = 2$.
7 a) $2y^3$
Divide the numbers, then divide the terms in y by subtracting the indices.
b) $8x^8$
Multiply the numbers, then multiply the terms in x by adding the indices.
b) $64y^6$
4^3 is 64, $(y^2)^3$ is $y^{2 \times 3}$
8 29.8 m/s
Substitute to find $\sqrt{12^2 - 2 \times (-9.8) \times 38}$
30 m/s
Substitute to find $\sqrt{10^2 - 2 \times (-10) \times 40}$.

9 $e = 0.6$
Substitute the values in the expression. The check also gives the answer 0.6.

6 Linear equations and formulae

The Check Up

1 a) $x = 3$
b) $x = 20$
c) $z = 4$
d) $y = 5$
e) $b = 7$
f) $x = 4$

2 a) $N = \frac{C - 5}{3}$
b) $b = \sqrt{\frac{V}{a}}$
c) $r = \frac{P - a}{\pi}$

3 a) $a < 2$
b) $b > -1$
c) $x \leqslant 10$
d) $-2 \leqslant a < 3$

Exam Practice

1 a) $70x$
b) $70p + 60q$
c) $70r + 180 = 460$
Work in the same units, pennies.
d) $r = 4$
Get rid of the '+ 180' by subtracting 180 from both sides, then get rid of the 'multiply by 70' by dividing both sides by 70.

2 $x = 5.5$
Remember the rectangle has four sides, so the perimeter is $2(x + 7 + x - 3)$, which leads to $2x + 4 = 15$, $2x = 11$.

3 a) $x = 8$
Get rid of the 'divide by 2', then get rid of the 'multiply by 9'.
b) $y = 3.5$
Get rid of the '+9' then the 'multiply by 4'.
c) $z = 4$
Get z on the left-hand side then get rid of the '+6'.

4 $x = 1.5$
Get rid of brackets first.

5 $x = 6$
Get rid of the + 7 first.

6 a) $x < 4$
Treat this as a linear equation, get rid of the '+1', then get rid of the 'multiply by 5'.
b) $x > 5$
Treat this as a linear equation, collect x-terms on the left-hand side and the numbers on the right-hand side.

7 $-2 \leqslant x < \frac{1}{3}$
Get rid of the '+4' by subtracting 4 on both sides, then get rid of the 'multiply by 3' by dividing by 3.

8 $P = \frac{C - 65}{7.5}$
Get rid of the '+ 65', then get rid of the 'multiply by 7.5'.

9 a) $V = 6.78 \times 10^4$
$V = 4.15 \times 10^5 \times 0.7^2 \div 3$
b) $y = \sqrt{\frac{3V}{x}}$
First get y^2 by itself, then take the square root to find y.

7 Factorising and quadratics

The Check Up

1 a) $40(3a + 1)$
b) $x(5x^2 - 1)$
c) $2x(5x + 3)$
d) $3pq^2(3q - 4p^2)$

2 a) $(x + 3)(x + 2)$
b) $(x - 2)(x + 5)$
c) $(a - 9)(a + 2)$
d) $(A - 5)(A - 4)$

3 a) $x = 12$ *or* $x = -2$
b) $q = 3$ *or* $q = -5$
c) $y = 0$ *or* $y = 3$

4 a) $x = +7$ or $x = -7$
b) $-2 \leqslant x \leqslant 2$

Exam Practice

1 $25(3A + 10)$
The first term is $25 \times 3 \times A$, the second term is 25×10.

2 $7x(x - 2)$
The first term is $7 \times x \times x$, the second term is $2 \times 7 \times x$.

3 a) $6a^2b^2(b - 2a)$
The first term is $6 \times a \times a \times b \times b$, the second term is $2 \times 6 \times a \times a \times a \times b \times b$.
b) $(x - 14)(x - 1)$
You want factor pairs of +14 which add to give −15.

4 a) $(x + 5)(x + 4)$
You want factor pairs of +20 which add to give +9.
b) $x = -5$ *or* $x = -4$
Solve $x + 5 = 0$, $x + 4 = 0$.

5 a) $x(x + 3)$
The first term is $x \times x$, second term is $3 \times x$.
b) $x = 0$ *or* $x = -3$
The first factor is x, the second factor is $x + 3$.

6 a) Area is $(x + 4)(x - 3) = x^2 + x - 12$
so $x^2 + x - 12 = 144$
Now subtract 144 from each side.
b) $x = 12$
$x^2 + x - 156 = (x + 13)(x - 12)$, x must be positive since it is a length, so $x = 12$.
c) 16 cm and 9 cm
12 + 4, 12 − 3

8 Plotting and using graphs

The Check Up

1 a)

x	−3	0	3
y	−14	−5	4

b)

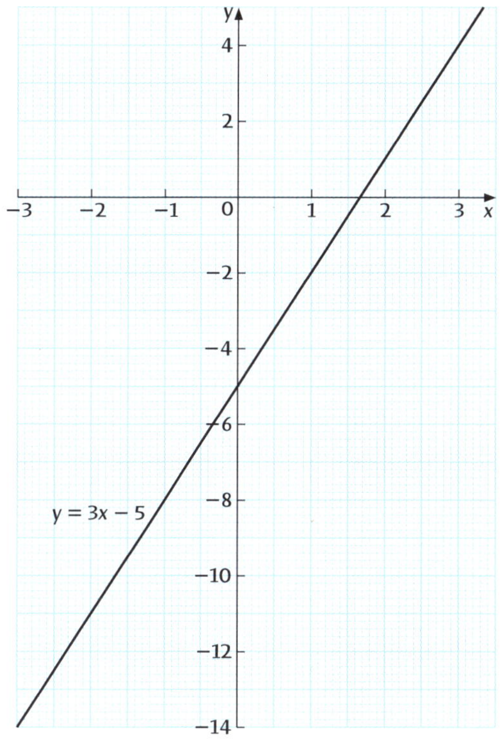

c) $x = 1.3$

2 a)

x	−2	−1	0	1	2	3
y	8	3	0	−1	0	3

b)

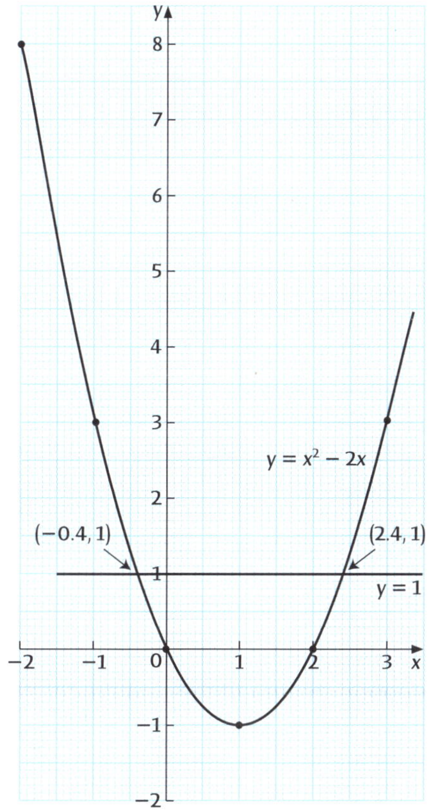

c) $x = 2.4$ or $x = -0.4$

d) $0 < x < 2$

3 a)

x	−3	0	3
$y = 2x + 4$	−2	4	10
$y = 2 - x$	5	2	−1

b)

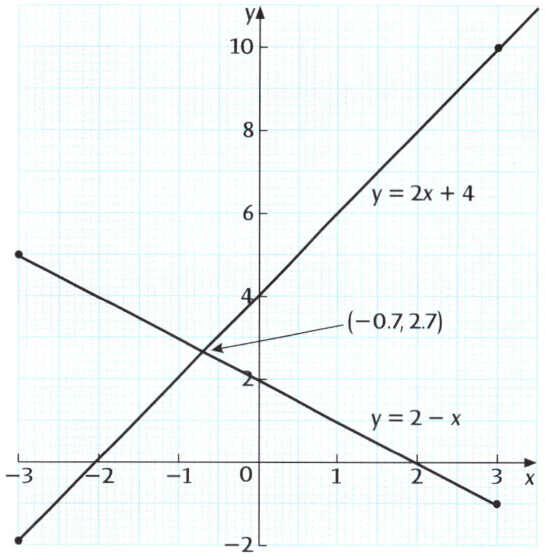

c) $x = -0.7$, $y = 2.7$

d) The solution of simultaneous equations $y = 2x + 4$ and $y = 2 - x$.

4

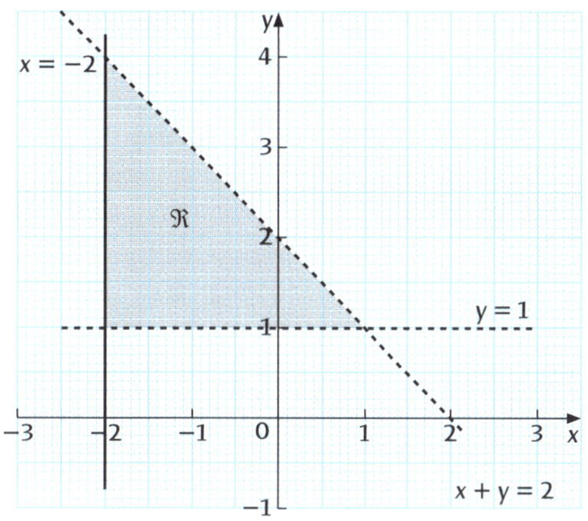

Exam Practice

1 a)

x	−1	0	1	2
y	−1	1	3	5

b)

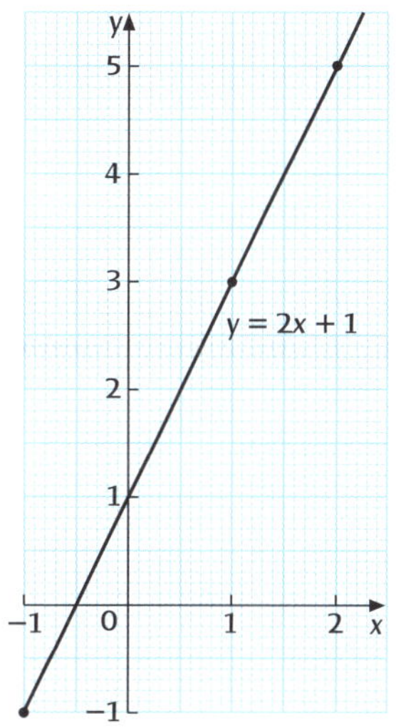

c) $x = 1.3$

2 a)

x	−3	−2	−1	0	1	2	3
y	8	3	0	−1	0	3	8

b)

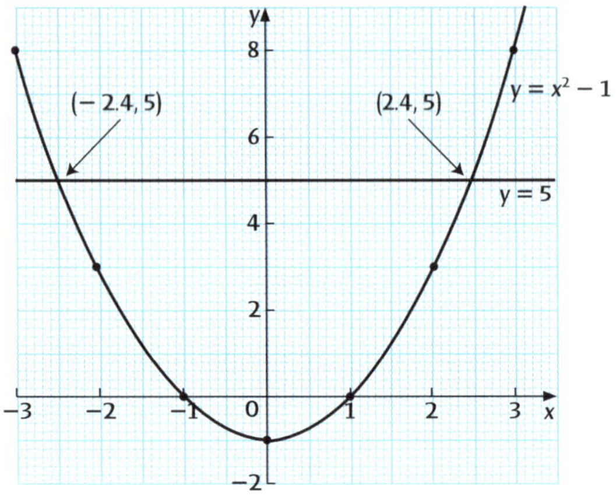

c) $x = +2.4$, $x = -2.4$

3 a)

x	−2	−1	0	1	2	3
y	11	5	1	−1	−1	1

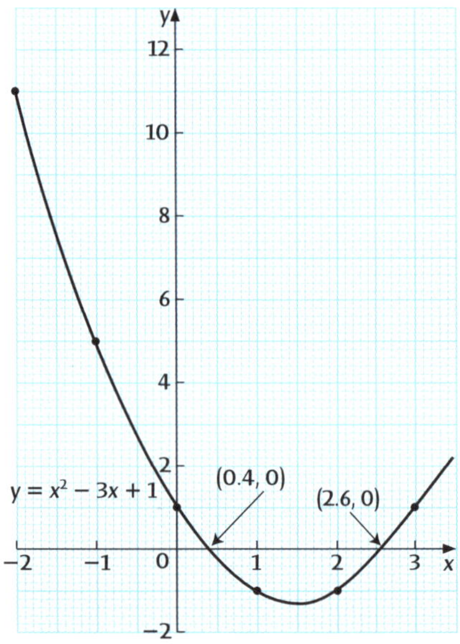

b) $x = 0.4$ or $x = 2.6$

c) $0.4 < x < 2.6$

d) -1.3

4 a)

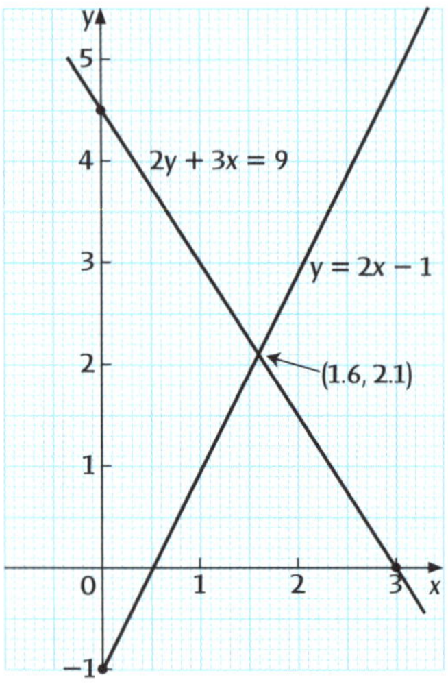

b) $x = 1.6$, $y = 2.1$

5 a)

x	−2	−1	0	1	2	3
y	−4	0	−2	−4	0	16

b)

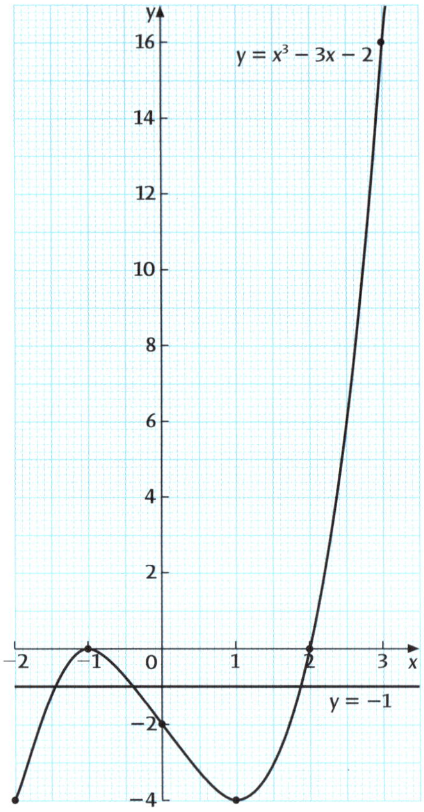

c) −1.4, −0.3, 1.9

6 $y \leqslant x$, $y > -1$, $x < 3$

9 Gradients and lines

The Check Up

1 a) $y = \frac{1}{2}x + 1$

b) $y = -\frac{2}{3}x + 2$

2 $y = 3x - 1$

3 The car stops 75 minutes from the start for 15 minutes. The greatest speed is 80 km/h.

4 Goss: the population increases at a constant rate from 1989 to 1999.

Den: at first the population declines quickly then the fall slows down until the population stabilises.

Exam Practice

1 a) £25

b) $y = \frac{1}{4}x + 25$

The intercept $c = 25$, then find the gradient m is $\frac{1}{4}$.

c) £62.50

Put $x = 150$ in $y = \frac{1}{4}x + 25$.

2 a) 12.18 a.m.

b) 12 minutes

c) 10.54 a.m.

d) 40 mph

e) Draw a line which finishes at Manchester at 3.00 p.m.

3 a) The line through (0, 8) and (4, 0).

b) $y = -2x + 8$

10 Solving more equations

The Check Up

1 $a = -2, b = 3$

2 $x = 1, y = 3$

3 $5c + 3t = 580, 4c + 5t = 620$
price of coffee $c = 80$, price of tea $t = 60$

4 $x = 2.74$

Exam Practice

1 $s = 4$
The two equations to solve are $l + s = 33$, $l - s = 25$.

2 $a = 5, \ b = -1$
Multiply the second equation by 2 to make the coefficient of b the same. As the signs are different, add the equations.

3 a) $20 = a + b, 30 = 3a + 9b$
Substitute $h = 20$ and $t = 1$ in $h = at + bt^2$ to find the first equation.
Substitute $h = 30$ and $t = 3$ in $h = at + bt^2$ to find the second equation: $30 = a \times 3 + b \times 3^2$
b) $a = 25, b = -5$
Multiply the first equation by 3 to make the a-coefficients the same, then subtract the equations.

4 $x = 3.5, y = \ -1$
To make the y−coefficients the same multiply the first equation by 2 and the second equation by 7. Then add the equations.

5 $x = 3.6$
Substitute $x = 4$ answer is too big, substitute $x = 3$ answer is too small. Substitute $x = 3.5$, answer is too small; $x = 3.6$, answer is too big. The solution lies between 3.55 and 3.6.

11 Sequences

The Check Up

1 a) 27, 33. The *n*th term is $6n - 3$.
b) −4, −7. The *n*th term is $11 - 3n$.
c) 125, 216. The *n*th term is n^3.

2 37, 50. The nth term is $n^2 + 1$.

3 21, 34

4 61, 80

Exam Practice

1 a) 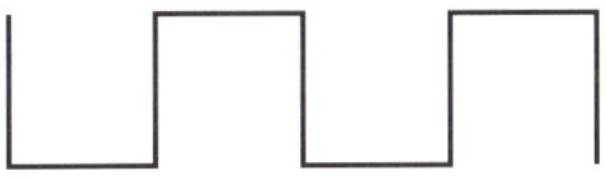
b) 9, 11, 13
c) $s = 1 + 2n$ or $2n + 1$
d) 201
Put $n = 100$ in the formula.

2 a) 
b) 16, 25, 36
c) 400
d) n^2
e) 27, 38; $n^2 + 2$

3 a) 14, 17, $3n - 1$
b) $\frac{5}{14}, \frac{6}{17}, \frac{n}{3n-1}$

4 23, 37

12 Angles and lines

The Check Up

1 123°, 65°, 105°

2 26°

3 130°

4 152°

5 51°

6 45°,135°; No, a regular octagon does not tessellate.

7 248°

Exam Practice

1 a) *p* is the alternate angle.
b) Angles at a point add up to 360°.

2 $r = 63°$
Base angles of an isosceles triangle.
$s = 54°$
The angles in a triangle add to 180°.
$t = 27°$
Find the angle next to s, then use the isosceles triangle property.

3 a) $u = 120°$
All the angles at the centre add up to 360°, so $u = 2 \times 360° \div 6 = 120°$.
$v = 60°$
The angle at the centre is 60° and AC = AB.
b) Equilateral
All the angles are 60°.
c) Yes
Each interior angle is 120° so you can fit three hexagons together without gaps.

4 a) 900°
Divide into five triangles.
b) $w = x = y = 130°$
Divide [900° − (175° + 155° + 90° + 90°)] by 3.
c) Obtuse
It is between 90° and 180°.

5 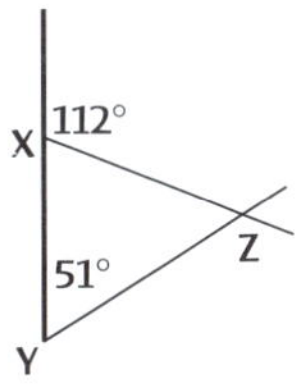

13 Transformations

The Check Up

1 a) Translation by $\begin{pmatrix} -11 \\ 5 \end{pmatrix}$
b) Rotation, centre (0, 0), anti-clockwise through 90°.
c) Reflection in the x-axis.
d) Reflection in the line $y = -x$.

2 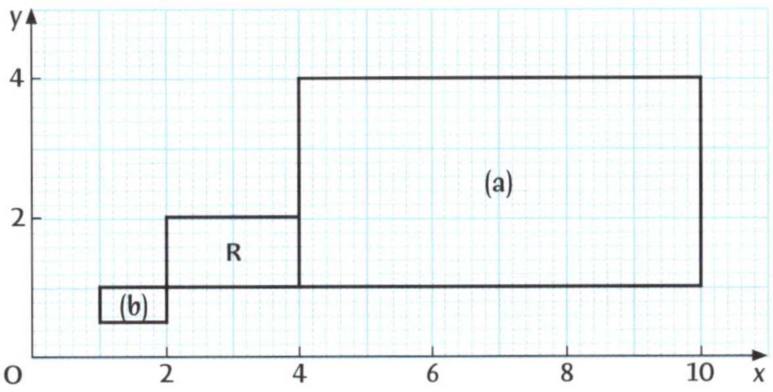

Exam Practice

1 a) (2, 4)

Join corresponding points in the object and image.

b) $\frac{1}{3}$

Calculate the fraction

$$\frac{\textit{length of side in image}}{\textit{length of corresponding side in object}}$$

2 a) Translation $\begin{pmatrix} 6 \\ 0 \end{pmatrix}$

Each point is moved 6 units in the positive (→) direction.

b) Reflection in the line y = −1

Every point in the object is the same distance as its corresponding point in the image from this line.

c) Rotation, centre (0, 0), 90° clockwise

Check with tracing paper.

3

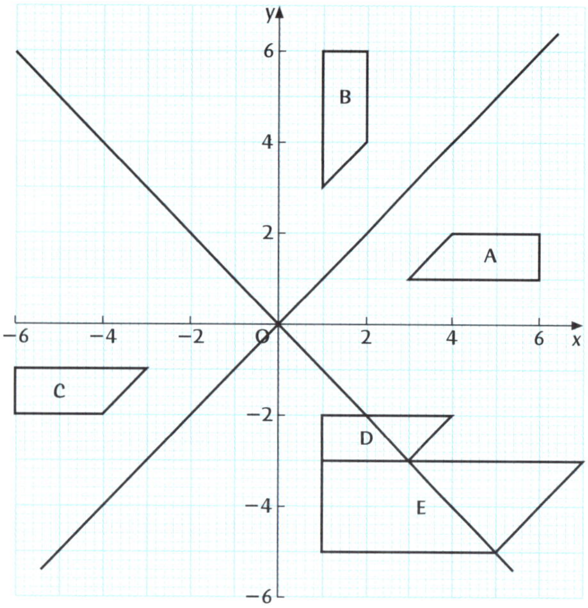

14 Loci

The Check Up

1 Draw the perpendicular bisector of the line AB.

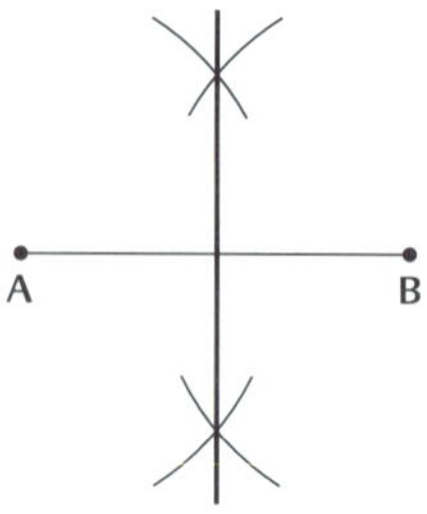

2 Draw a line and construct its perpendicular bisector, as above.

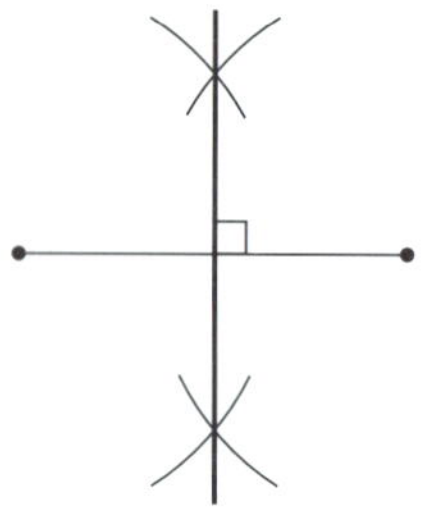

3

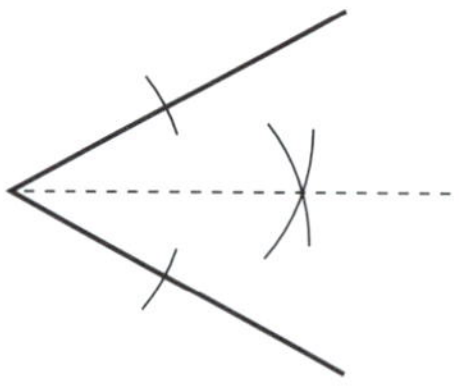

Exam Practice

1

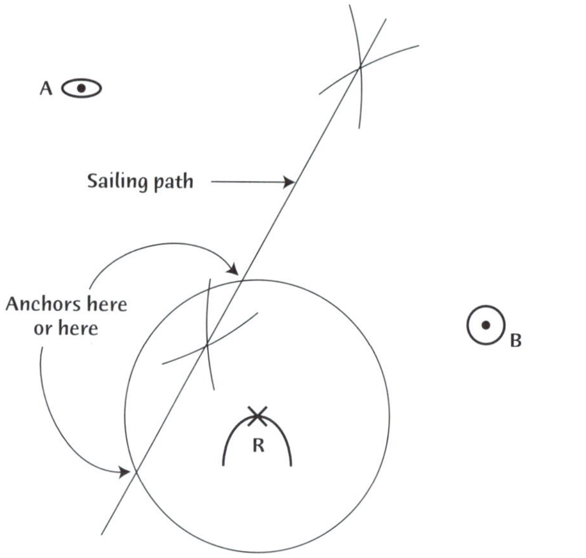

Draw the perpendicular bisector of AB for the sailing path between A and B.

Draw a circle centre R radius 1.5 cm. The boat anchors where the arc intersects the perpendicular bisector.

2

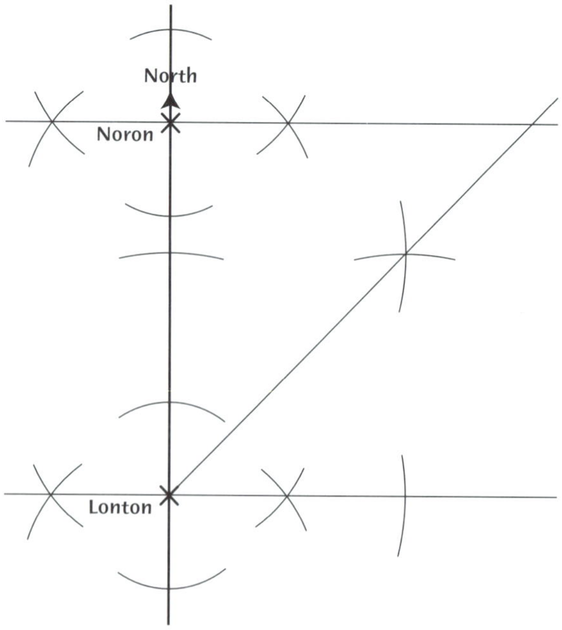

Construct an angle of 45° at Lonton by bisecting a right angle and construct an angle of 90° at Noron. Oxdon is where these intersect.

3

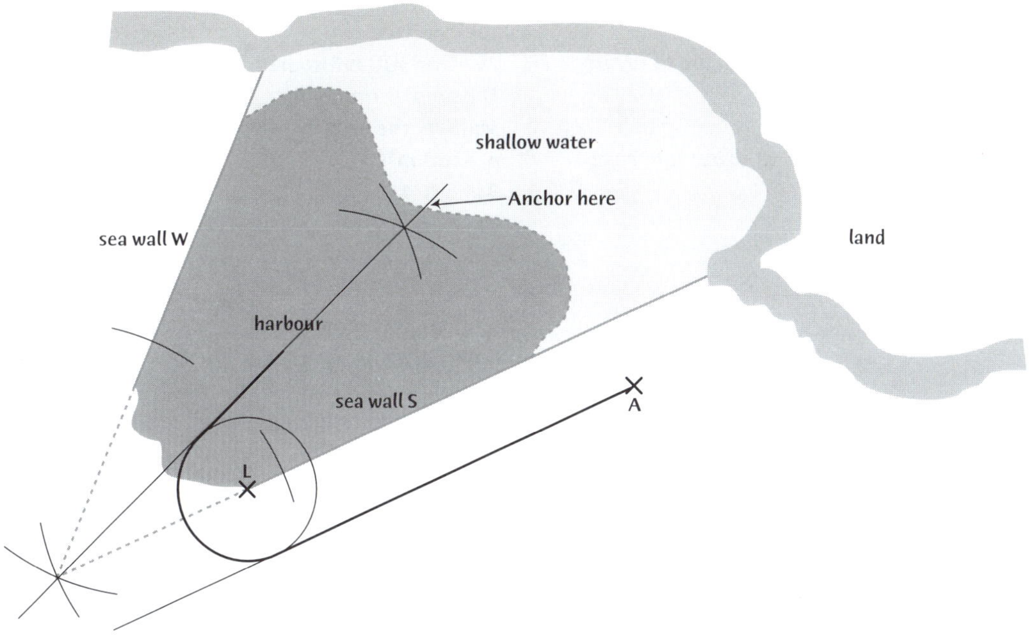

Draw a line 1 cm from S, then a circle centre L radius 1 cm. Next construct the bisector of the angle formed where the sea walls meet, stop in shallow water.

15 Triangles

The Check Up

1 9.53 cm

2 11.3 cm

3 Yes, $3^2 = 2.4^2 + 1.8^2$

4 a) Corresponding angles: ∠ABC = ∠ADE, ∠ACB = ∠AED, ∠A is common

b) 5 cm

5 a) Alternate angles: ∠WVX = ∠XYZ, ∠VWX = ∠YZX
Opposite angles ∠WXV = ∠YXZ

b) 4.2 cm

Exam Practice

1 18.0 km

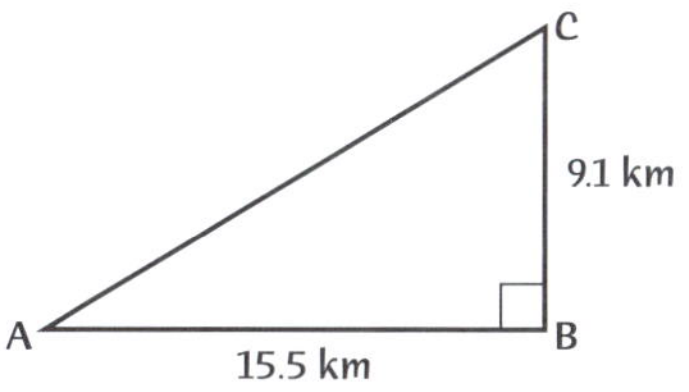

You want the long side so square and add, then take the square root of $(9.1^2 + 15.5^2)$.

2 a) 16.5 cm
You want the short side so square and subtract, then take the square root of $(21^2 - 13^2)$.

b) 26.4 cm
You want the long side so square and add, then take the square root of $(16^2 + 21^2)$.

3 a) 65°
Corresponding angles: ∠TPR = ∠SQR
so $180° - (30° + 85°)$.

b) 11.7 cm
The ratios are $\frac{PR}{5} = \frac{7}{3}$.

c) 4.7 cm
The ratios are $\frac{SR}{11} = \frac{3}{7}$.

4 a) 15 cm
$\frac{AC}{BC} = \frac{5}{1}$ *so the ratios are* $\frac{AE}{3} = \frac{5}{1}$

b) 52 cm
The ratios are $\frac{EC}{13} = \frac{5}{1}$, *and* $ED = EC - DC$.

5 a) ∠PSR and ∠SQR are both 90°. ∠PRS is the same for both triangles.
The triangles have equal angles so they are similar.

b) 12.8 cm
The ratios are $\frac{PR}{8} = \frac{8}{5}$.

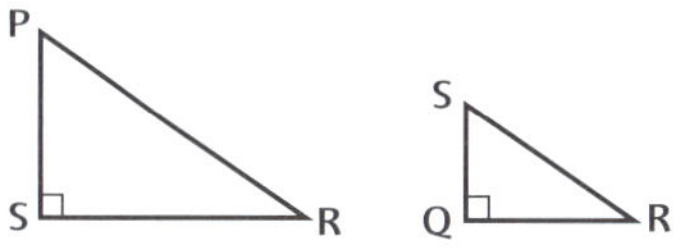

16 Trigonometry

The Check Up

1 34.2°

2 9.17 cm

3 15.7 cm

4 38.5°

Exam Practice

1 2.53 m
You want 'o', you have 'a' so use tan.

2 41.4°
You have 'a' and 'h' so use cos. To find the value of the angle use the shift or second function.

3 311.4°
First find the angle at Shefford, using tan and the shift or second function key. The bearing is $360° - 48.6°$.

4 a) 4.3(5) m
You have 'h', you want 'a' so use cos.

b) 1.15 m or 1.2 m
Use Pythagoras' theorem.

c) 22.5°
You have 'o' and 'h', so use sin. To find the value of the angle use the shift or second function key.

d) 10.6 m
First use Pythagoras' theorem to find TB.

5 a) 9.20 m
You have 'o', you want 'a' so use tan. Take care to divide by tan 41°.
b) 16.97 m = 17.0 m
First find VX: you have 'o', you want 'a' so use tan. Take care to divide by tan 17°.

17 Length and area

The Check Up

1 14.3 cm
2 558
3 52 m, 81 m^2
4 a) 9.8 square inches
b) 7.5 cm^2
c) 11.3 m^2
5 100.8 square feet

Exam Practice

1 a) 25 cm^2
Use the formula for the area of a trapezium.
$A = \frac{1}{2}(3 + 7) \times 5$ cm²
b) 21.4 cm
x is the 'long' side so $x = \sqrt{5^2 + 4^2}$. Remember to go all the way round.
2 a) 8.0 cm
Divide by π to get r^2, then take the square root to get r.
b) 550 cm^2
Find (area of outer circle − area of yellow circle).
3 a) 64.8 cm
Remember to add all four sides.
b) 170 cm^2
First find the height using the trigonometric sin ratio. Area is base × height.
4 a) 30.8 m or 3080 cm
The perimeter is (half circumference + 1200) cm, remember to work in m or cm for all lengths.
b) 154
To find the number of plants divide the perimeter by 20.
c) 56.5 m^2
The area is half the area of a circle.
d) 4
To find the number of boxes divide the area by 14.
5 a) 2135 cm^2
The area is $\frac{1}{2} \times 70 \times 61$ cm².
b) 343 cm^2
Don t count the centre of the cross twice.
c) 1792 cm^2
You need to find (area of sign − area of cross).

18 3D shapes

The Check Up

1 6 m^3, 4500 l
2 c = 5 cm, 600 cm^3
3 0.427 l, 46
4 54 cm^2
5 31 cm
6 a) volume b) area c) area
d) area e) length f) volume

Exam Practice

1 292.5 or 300 m^3 (to nearest 10 m^3)
The area of triangular cross-section is $\frac{1}{2} \times 10 \times 4.5$. Multiply the area by 13.25 to find the volume.
2 a) 160 m^3
$8 \times 5 \times 4$
b) Here are two possible answers.

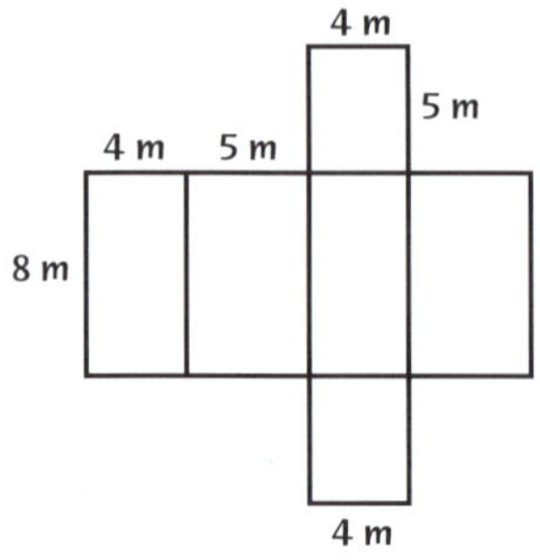

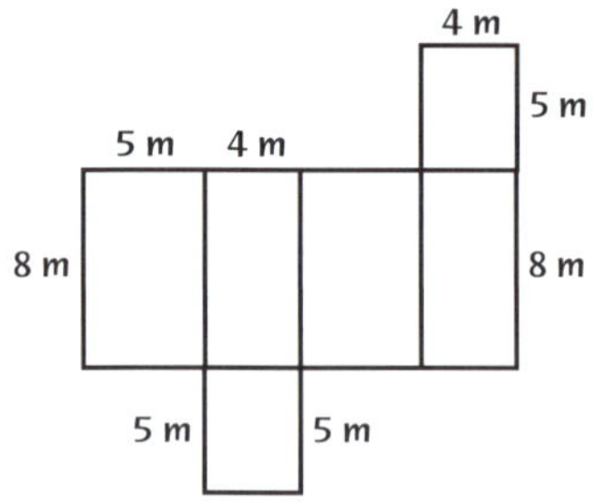

c) 2, 8, 10 or 4, 4, 10
Or any other factors of 160.
d) 4, 5, 10
The new volume is 200 so choose factors of 200.
e) 184 m^2
The total surface area is 2 × area of front + 2 × area of side + 2 × area of top.
3

or

4 a) 578 cm^3
Remember to use radius².
b) 24
You can fit 4 cans along the width and 6 along the length.
c) 23 cm
Twice the height of one can.
d) 35 328 cm^3
$23 \times 48 \times 32$
e) 7584 cm^3
You need to find the volume of the box − 48 × the volume of one can.
5 $2\pi h(r + R)$
Because it has [length]² which are units for area.
6 48.8 cm or 49 cm to 2 s.f.
Multiply litres by 1000 so you can work in the same units. Then radius² is volume ÷ (40 × π). Multiply the radius by 2 for the diameter.

19 Data

The Check Up

1 40°, 50, 10%
2 Angles are 72°, 48°, 96°, 24°, 120°

3

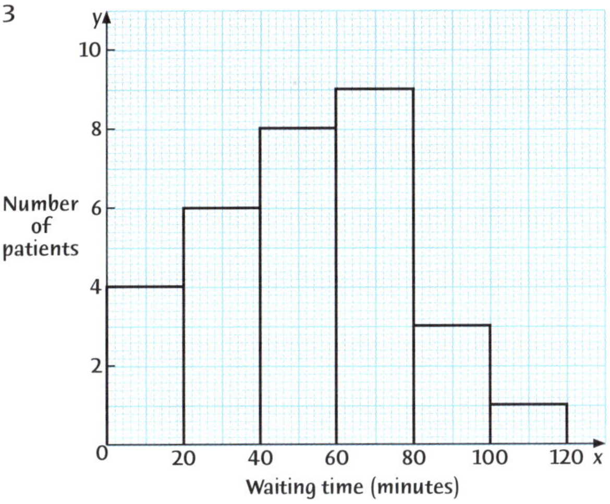

4

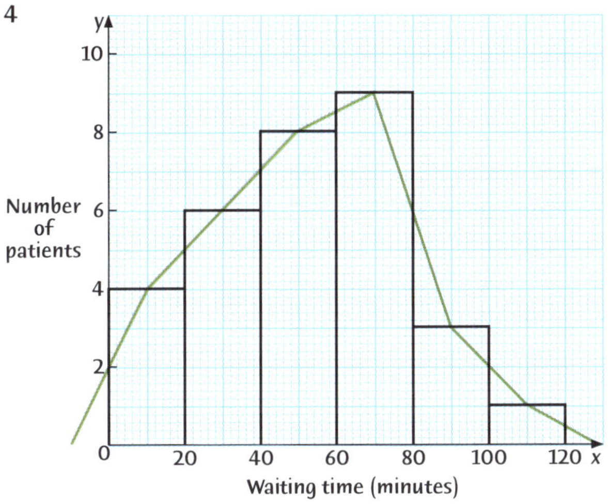

Join the middles of the bars in the histogram, and extend to the axis on both sides.

Exam Practice

1

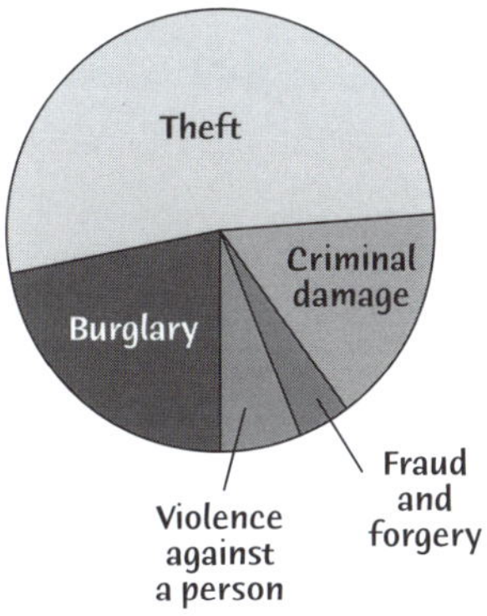

The angles are 79°, 187°, 58°, 14°, 22°. 1% is represented by 3.6°.

2

Weight	Frequency

Group the weights into classes of equal intervals. Make up the frequency table using tallies.

3 a) £5400

The angle is 180° so the sector is half the total amount.

b) £2700

The angle is 90° so quarter total amount.

c) 40°

The fraction is $\frac{1200}{10\,800}$ *of total amount.*

$y = 50°$

The total of all the angles must be 360°.

4 a)

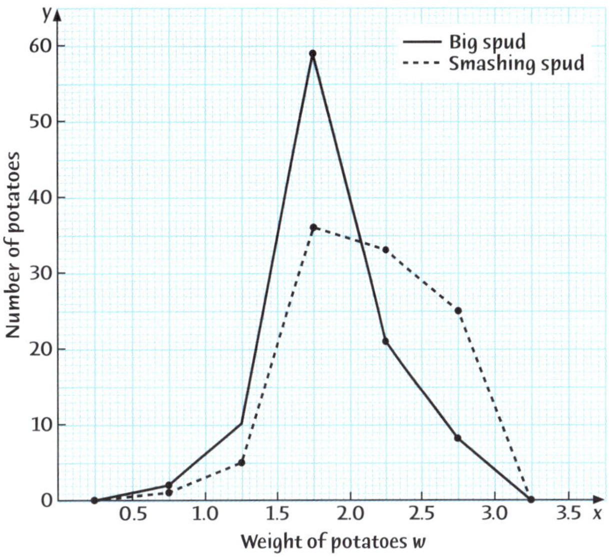

Plot the middle of each interval against the frequency.

b) Smashing spud

There are more potatoes in the heavier classes.

c) Big spud

There are more variation of numbers of potatoes in each class.

20 Averages and ranges

The Check Up

1 a) 6 b) 5 c) 5.27 d) 9

2 a) 40 to 60 years

b) 20 to 40 years

c) 37.7 years or 37 years 8 months 12 days

3 a) 28 b) 38, 20 c) 18 d) 14

Exam Practice

1 a) 5.2

The sum of all the shoe sizes is 310.5.

b) 5

The middle (30th) size occurs in size 5 class.

c) 5.5

This is the size that occurs most often.

d) It would be more useful to use the mode, the size which occurs most often.

2 a)

Journey time t in minutes	Number of children f	Cumulative frequency c.f.
$0 \leq t < 10$	8	8
$10 \leq t < 20$	14	22
$20 \leq t < 30$	25	47
$30 \leq t < 40$	35	82
$40 \leq t < 60$	11	93
$60 \leq t < 80$	5	98
$80 \leq t < 120$	2	100

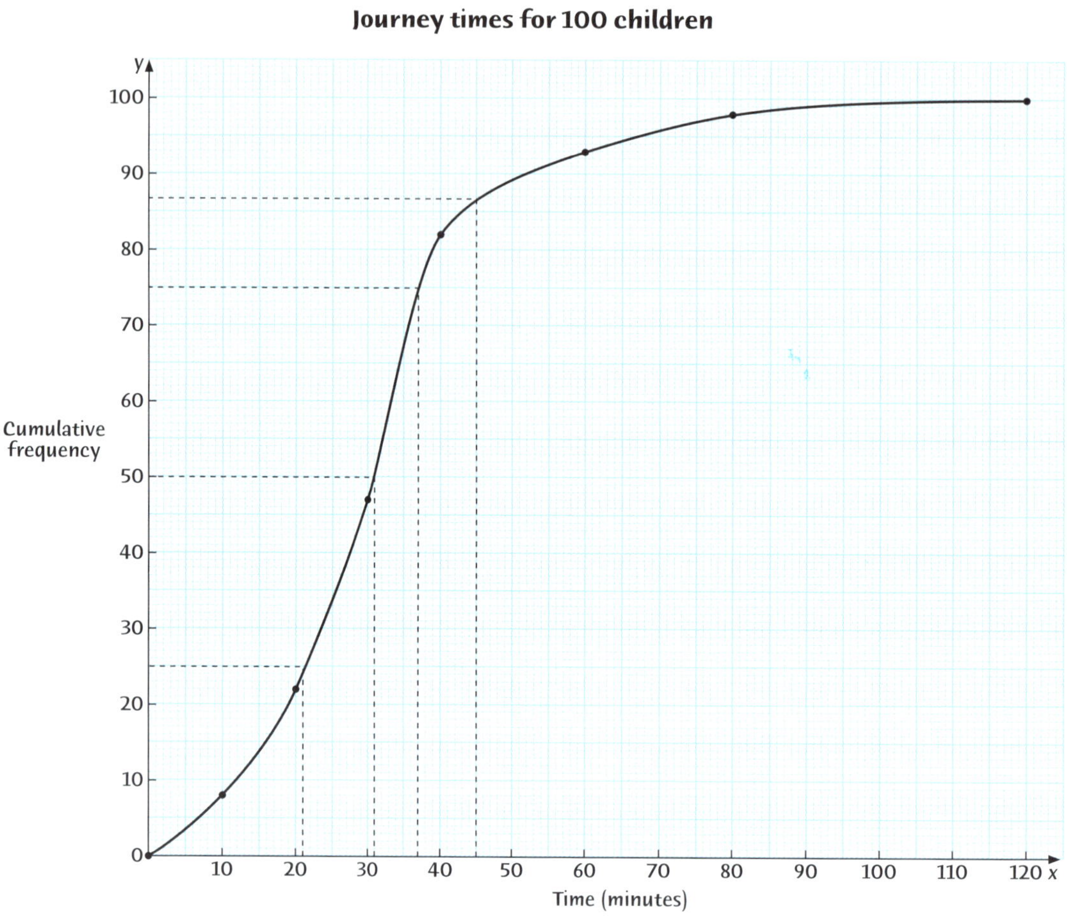

Plot the top of range of data against cumulative frequency: (10, 8), (20, 22), (30, 47), (40, 82), (60, 93), (80, 98), (120, 100).

b) 31 minutes

Find 50 on the cumulative frequency axis, go across to the curve and then down to journey time.

c) 37, 21

Start from the cumulative frequency axis at 75 for UQ and at 25 for LQ.

d) 16 small because most journeys are close to the median

IQR = UQ − LQ

e) 13%

Find 45 minutes on the time axis, go up to curve then across to the cumulative frequency axis. The number of children with times more than 45 minutes is 100 − 87 = 13.

3 32 minutes

Use the middle of the class interval. The sum of all the times is 3200 minutes. Estimate because you can assume all results lie in the middle of the class.

21 Scatter diagrams

The Check Up

1

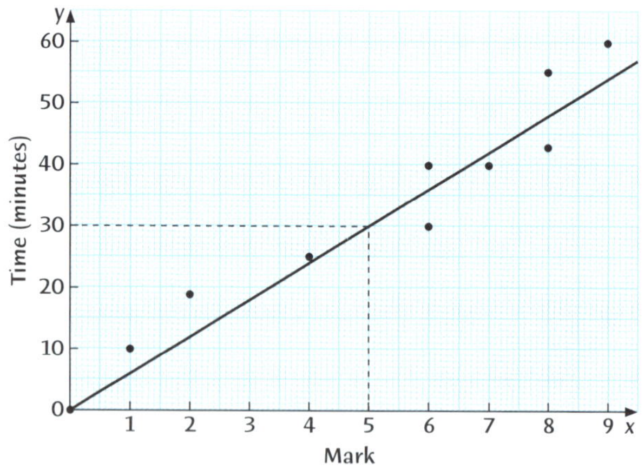

There is fairly strong positive correlation.

2 30 minutes

3 This is outside the range of data and would give a mark more than 10.

Exam Practice

1 a) No correlation

b) Weak negative correlation

2 a) 3.9 cm

The sum of all the data is 46.5; divide by 12.

b), c)

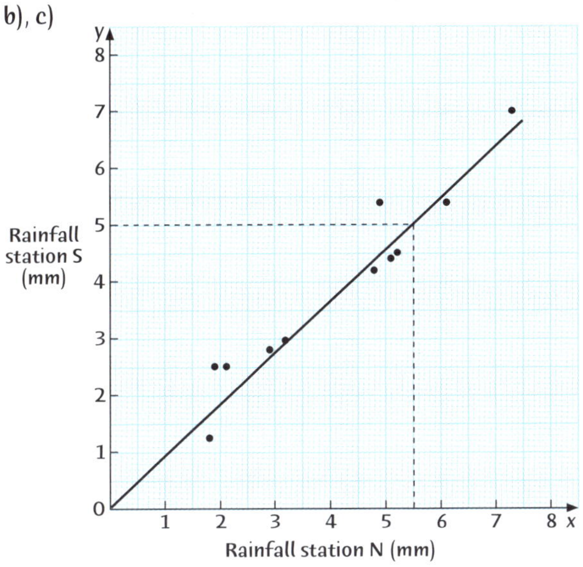

d) Strong positive

Most points are on or near the line of best fit, which has a positive gradient.

e) 5.5 cm

Start at 5 cm on S, go across to line then down to 5.5 cm on N.

22 Probability

The Check Up

1 0.65

2 0.15

3 a) $\frac{9}{20}$ b) $\frac{14}{20}$ or $\frac{7}{10}$ c) $\frac{15}{20}$ or $\frac{3}{4}$

4 8

5 0.4125

6

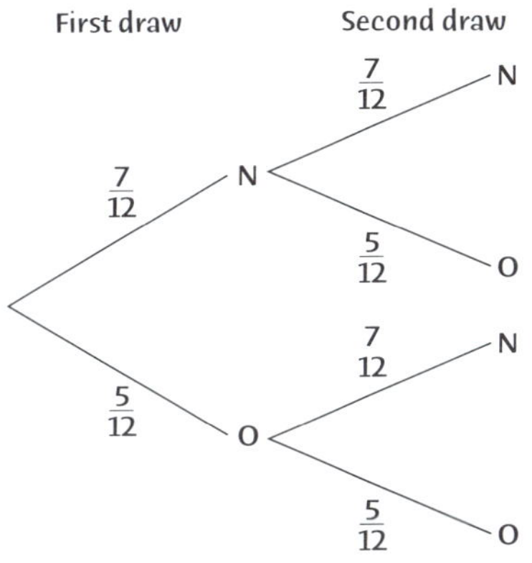

a) $\frac{35}{144}$ b) $\frac{70}{144} = \frac{35}{72}$ c) $\frac{119}{144}$

Exam Practice

1 a) 0.45

Use the first 1 rule.

b) 27

Calculate 12 × 5 × probability of train not on time.

2 a)

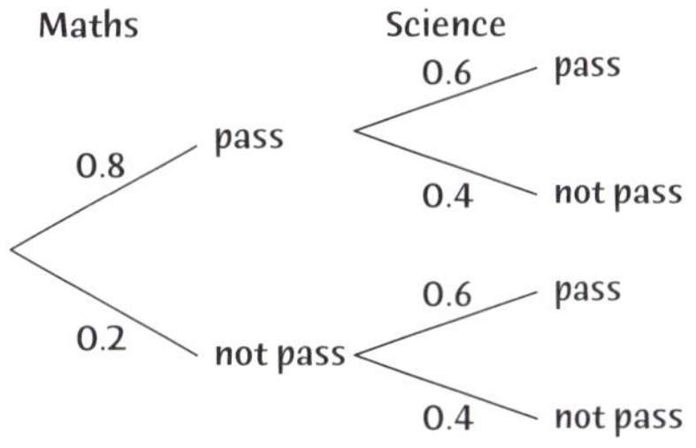

b) 0.48

You want 'pass' and 'pass' so multiply 0.8 × 0.6.

c) 0.44

You want 'pass M' and 'not pass S' or 'not pass M' and 'pass S' so add 0.8 × 0.4 + 0.2 × 0.6.

3 a) 0.25

You want the probability of a 2.

b) $\frac{3}{16}$ or 0.1875

You want to throw 1 and 4, or 3 and 2, or 4 and 1, so calculate $\frac{1}{4} \times \frac{1}{4} + \frac{1}{4} \times \frac{1}{4} + \frac{1}{4} \times \frac{1}{4} = \frac{3}{16}$ *(0.1875).*

4 a) 0.2

b) 0.6

Add all probabilities for a square and probabilities for 3.

c) 0.5

Add all probabilities of a triangle and all probabilities for 2. Take care not to count the 'triangular and 2' disc twice.

d) 80

Total of all probabilities of scoring 1 are 0.2 so 16 discs represent 0.2 of the total number. Therefore the total number of discs is 16 ÷ 0.2 = 80.

5

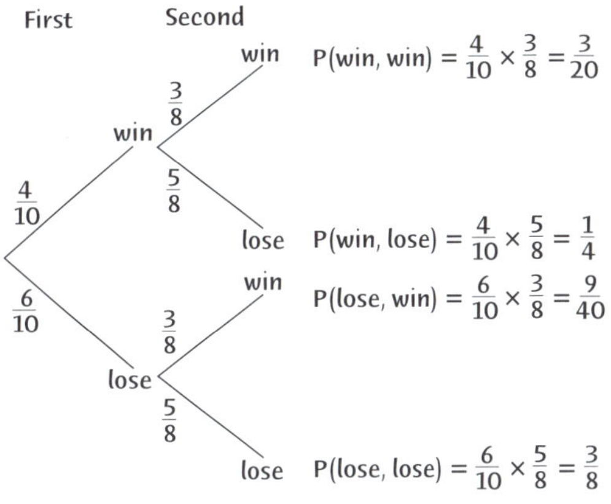

a) $\frac{3}{20}$

You want 'win' and 'win' so multiply: $\frac{4}{10} \times \frac{3}{8}$.

b) $\frac{19}{40}$

You want 'win first dip' and 'not win second dip' or 'not win first dip' and 'win second dip' so add $\frac{4}{10} \times \frac{5}{8} + \frac{6}{10} \times \frac{3}{8}$.

c) $\frac{5}{8}$

You want (1 – probability of not winning).

Text © Liz Hamilton 2000
Illustrations © Stanley Thornes (Publishers) 2000

The right of Liz Hamilton to be identified as the author of this work has been asserted by her in accordance with the Copyright, Designs and Patents Act 1988.

All rights reserved. No part of this publication may be reproduced or transmitted in any form or by any means, electronic or mechanical, including photocopy, recording or any information storage or retrieval system, without permission in writing from the publisher or under licence from the Copyright Licensing Agency Limited. Further details of such licences (for reprographic reproduction) may be obtained from the Copyright Licensing Agency Limited of 90 Tottenham Court Road, London W1P 9HE.

This edition published exclusively for WHSmith, 2000, by:
Stanley Thornes (Publishers) Ltd
Ellenborough House
Wellington Street
CHELTENHAM GL50 1YW

00 01 02 03 04 / 10 9 8 7 6 5 4 3 2 1

A catalogue record for this book is available from the British Library.

ISBN 0-7487-5490-3

Designed by Rocket Design Ltd, London
Typeset by Tech-Set Ltd, Gateshead, Tyne & Wear
Printed and bound in Italy by G.Canale & C.S.p.A., Borgaro T.se, Turin